Footprints
of the
Fisherman

Carol Ruvolo

*Life Lessons From One Who
Walked Closely With Christ*

DEO VOLENTE

PUBLISHING

Carol Ruvolo, *Footprints of the Fisherman*
©2001 by Carol Ruvolo.
Published by Deo Volente Publishing
            P.O. Box 4847
            Los Alamos, NM 87544

Printed in the United States of America.

Scripture taken from the NEW AMERICAN STANDARD BIBLE ®, © Copyright The Lockman Foundation 1960, 1962, 1968, 1971, 1973, 1975, 1977, 1995
Used by permission

Appendices A and B are from *Turning on the Light* by Carol Ruvolo. They are used by permission from P & R Publishing.

ISBN: 0-9658804-7-8

Table of Contents

For Diana Hunt,
a dear friend
who walks very closely with Christ

"To ask that God's love should be content with us as we are is to ask that God should cease to be God."

C. S. Lewis

Preface

If you are familiar with the New Testament Gospels, you know that a brash, rugged fisherman named Simon Peter walked very closely with our Lord Jesus Christ. One of my favorite Bible teachers summed up Peter's closeness to Christ in this memorable word picture: "I am sure that every time the Lord Jesus slowed down or stopped suddenly, the Apostle Peter ran right into the back of Him." From the moment his brother Andrew brought him to the Messiah until he watched Jesus ascend to the right hand of the Father, this brash, rugged fisherman dogged His Lord's steps.

Simon Peter loved Jesus Christ with all of his heart, soul, mind, and strength — but he loved Him imperfectly because he was human. Although Peter was wholly committed to Christ, he did many things wrong. There must have been days when he wondered if he'd ever make it. I'm a lot like that, and you probably are too. That's why we identify with Peter so well, and have so much to learn from his example.

This study focuses on Peter's relationship with the Lord Jesus Christ. Each chapter deals with a critical episode in their relationship from which we can draw some valuable life lessons. The study questions at the end of each lesson will encourage us to apply what we learn from Peter's example in our daily lives.

Seeking to walk in the footprints of the fisherman requires a worthwhile investment of time and energy. The Westminster Shorter Catechism declares that fulfilling our chief end of glorifying and enjoying God is inextricably linked to "doing the Word" (See Q/A 1 & 2). Thus, if we want to walk worthy of our high calling in Christ (and we do!), we must *make an effort* to understand and apply the great truths of the Bible. Many of those truths are exemplified in the lives of faithful disciples like Simon the fisherman. Getting to know him more intimately and striving to walk as he walked will help us fulfill the chief end for which we were created.

Before undertaking this study, you should know that I believe in and unashamedly teach the plenary inspiration, infallibility, inerrancy, authority, and sufficiency of the Bible. I am also convinced that Reformed theology is the clearest and most accurate human restatement of God's revelation in Scripture.

If you are new to Bible study or are uncertain about the inspiration, infallibility, inerrancy, authority, or sufficiency of Scripture, please lay this study aside and investigate the validity of the truth claims the Bible makes for itself.[1] You will benefit more fully from Bible study when you understand the *uniqueness* of God's revelation in Scripture. If you are unfamiliar with the term "Reformed Theology," please read Appendix A, "What is Reformed Theology?" before beginning this study.

Bible study is a serious task that requires physical, mental, and spiritual preparation to be done well. Study when you are well-rested and alert. Establish a time and place that is quiet, free of distractions, and conducive to concentration. Get in the habit of taking notes on what you read, and develop a filing system that will enable you to access those notes in the future. Expect Bible study to challenge you and stretch your thinking. Expect it to be difficult at times — but extremely rewarding. Always begin your study time in prayer. Ask the Lord to reveal sin in your life that needs to be confessed and cleansed, to help you concentrate on His truths, and to help you understand what He has written. End your study with a prayer for opportunities to *apply* what you have learned and for the wisdom to recognize those opportunities when they occur.

Remember that Bible study equips you *to glorify God and enjoy Him forever.* You glorify God when your thoughts, words, attitudes, and actions accurately reflect God's character and nature to those around you. You enjoy God when you are fully satisfied and content in His providential ordering of the circumstances of your life. When your life consistently glorifies God and your joy is rooted in His sovereign providence, your impact on our fallen world will be nothing short of tremendous.

Each lesson in this study is followed by three types of questions: **Review**, **Applying the Word**, and **Digging Deeper**. The *Review* questions will help you determine how well you understood the lesson material by challenging you to express the key points of the lesson in your own words. *Applying the Word* questions encourage you to put your understanding of the lesson to work in your daily life, and

Digging Deeper questions challenge you to pursue further study in certain areas.

You should be able to find the answers to the *Review* questions in the lesson material itself, but please resist the temptation to copy words or phrases out of the book. Work hard at putting these ideas into your own words. Being able to do this indicates that you have *understood* what you have read. Ask yourself, "How would I explain this idea to someone else if I didn't have the book with me?"

Try to answer at least one of the *Applying the Word* questions. If you do not have time to answer all of them, pray over them and ask the Lord to show you which one(s) *He* wants you to work on. These applications should take some time and thought because, to be effective, they must be answered specifically instead of in vague generalities.

An example illustrating the difference between vague generalities and specific applications might be helpful here. If you are applying the truths found in Philippians 2:3-4 about regarding others as more important than yourself by looking out for their interests, a vague generality would be: "I need to be more helpful and kind to those around me." A specific application would be: "I will call my daughter this morning (who lives in a sorority house on the local college campus) and cheerfully offer to edit her term paper while she studies for her final exams. If she accepts my offer, I will do my Saturday chores on Friday, leaving Saturday free to help her." Do you see the difference? A specific application answers the questions:

Who? My daughter.

What? Call her, volunteer to edit her paper, and reschedule my chores.

When? Call this morning at 10AM, edit the paper on Saturday, and do the chores on Friday.

Where? Call from my home. Edit the paper at her sorority house library.

How? Cheerfully.

A vague generality does not answer these questions. You can make specific applications in the areas of your thinking, your attitudes, and your behavior. (See Lesson 6 of my Light for Your Path study, *Turning on the Light* for more information about how to make specific applications.)

Digging Deeper questions usually require a significant amount of time and effort to complete. They were designed to provide a challenge for Christians who are eager for more advanced study. Don't assume that you are "supposed" to do all (or any) of these. Read them, and if you find one that intrigues you, spend several weeks (or several months!) working on it. You may end up writing a book of your own.

As you get to know Simon Peter as you work through this study, remember that your motivation should be growth in Christlikeness for the glory of God. Growth requires you to stretch beyond where you are now. Spiritual stretching is often painful and difficult, but it is always rewarding. If you need help with your work, ask your pastor, one of your church leaders, or a mature Christian friend to work with you. They will almost assuredly be delighted to do so.

If you are doing this study with a group, please resist the temptation to compare yourself with other Christians in the group. Do not be intimated by someone whose notebook is bulging with insightful answers to every question, and do not feel superior to someone who struggled to answer only one or two questions. Rather, bear in mind that growth in Christlikeness occurs as we learn and apply God's truth "a little here, a little there" (Isaiah 28:10), and that we do not all grow at the same rate or in the same way. The issue is not how many questions you answered or how well you expressed yourself. The issue is whether or not you have moved beyond where you were when you started the lesson. If you have, you are growing. And that's why you are studying!

May our great God richly bless your diligent efforts to learn from Simon's example and to walk in his footprints.

Notes:

1. The following books are among the many helpful resources that will help you investigate the claims the Bible makes for itself:

James M. Boice, *Standing On the Rock*. Grand Rapids: Baker Books, 1994.

R. Will Butler, *God Speaks:What the Bible Teaches About Itself*. Los Alamos, N.M.: Deo Volente Publishing

John MacArthur, Jr., *You Can Trust the Bible*. Chicago: Moody Press, 1988.

Josh McDowell, *Evidence That Demands a Verdict*. San Bernardino, CA: Here's Life Publishers, Inc., 1972, 1979.

Carol J. Ruvolo, *A Book Like No Other: What's So Special About the Bible*. Phillipsburg, N. J.: P & R Publishing Co., 1998.

R. C. Sproul, *Explaining Inerrancy*. Orlando Fla.: Ligonier Ministries, 1980, 1996.

B. B. Warfield, *The Inspiration and Authority of the Bible*. Phillipsburg, N.J.: Presbyterian and Reformed Publishing Co., 1948.

*"The secret of Christian influence
is the society of the Christian's Master."*

࿐

Hugh Martin

Chapter 1

Peter's Footprints All Lead to Christ

At the time of Christ, most people knew that "all roads led to Rome." That's because Rome built those roads as a means of maintaining world rule by tightly controlling commerce and government. Rome's roads were an integral part of the seemingly solid foundation upon which her empire rested. But like all worldly support systems, it had fatal flaws. And those flaws allowed those very roads to be used by the hoards of barbarians who eventually overthrew one of the world's greatest Empires. All roads still led to Rome for awhile after her fall, but tragically, there was no longer any real reason to go there.

In much the same way (but with one stunning exception), the example of faithful saints all lead to God. Their lives, their words, and their prayers direct us toward the way, the truth, and the life. As they exercise the rich gifts of God's Spirit and pour themselves out in worship and service, the sweet aroma of the knowledge of Him is dispersed in every place. They leave footprints for us that point out the narrow way of faith in Christ Jesus which alone leads to God. And as we walk in those footprints, we leave footprints for others.

The examples of one group of those faithful saints — the apostles and prophets — form the foundation of God's church in the world. Jesus Christ is the cornerstone of that foundation. As such, He gives His Church the solid, attractive integrity that makes it the glorious dwelling of God's Holy Spirit. The foundation comprised of the apostles and prophets and one perfect cornerstone supports the Church much as Rome's roads supported her Empire — except that it has no fatal flaws. That's because it's comprised of God's inspired revelation: the Incarnate Christ and the writings of Scripture. The foundation that God has laid down for His Church is perfectly solid and unable to crack. It will support without fail what He builds upon it.

God builds His Church upon the foundation of the apostles and prophets through the work of His people who submit to His Spirit. That's why Paul advises us in 1 Corinthians to be careful how we build upon that foundation. "Now if any man builds upon the foundation with gold, silver, precious stones, wood, hay, straw, each man's work will become evident; for the day will show it, because it is to be revealed with fire; and the fire itself will test the quality of each man's work. If any man's work which he has built upon it remains, he shall receive a reward. If any man's work is burned up, he shall suffer loss; but he himself shall be saved, yet so as through fire. Do you not know that you are a temple of God, and that the Spirit of God dwells in you?" (3:12-16).

What a privilege to be involved in building God's church in the world! As we add walls, rooms, furnishings, and adornments to His perfect foundation, we glorify God as we rely on His power and reflect His attributes. But with that great privilege comes great responsibility. When we fail to submit to God's Holy Spirit, we build upon God's foundation with wood, hay, and straw — worldly, self-reliant materials that do not display the glory of God. Only the works of obedience will shine as gold, silver, and precious stones reflecting God's nature in our fallen world.

All of us want the work that we do in the church to withstand the refining fire of God's judgment. None of us want to see years of hard work go up in smoke on judgment day. How can we be encouraged to be steadfast, immovable, always abounding in the work of the Lord, knowing that our toil is not in vain in the Lord? There is only one way. By studying God's Word and applying His truth in our daily lives. The examples of faithful saints recorded in Scripture will help us to do that.

A Pattern for Discipleship

Almost two thousand years ago, a small group of men stood on a mountain with the resurrected Lord Jesus and listened while He issued His Church her marching orders: "All authority has been given to Me in heaven and on earth. Go therefore and make disciples of all the nations, baptizing them in the name of the Father and the Son and the Holy Spirit, teaching them to observe all that I commanded you; and lo, I am with you always, even to the end of the age" (Matthew 28:18-20).

In the Greek language this Great Commission contains one imperative verb and three participles, indicating that Jesus was issuing a single command along with instructions about how to fulfill it. The command is "make disciples," and the instructions are "go," "baptize," and "teach." Jesus also infused the Commission with profound motivation by affirming that He had been given all authority in heaven and on earth, and that He would be with them until the end of the age.

The men who heard these words from the mouth of our Lord knew precisely *what* they were to do, *how* they were to do it, and *why* they must do it. They were to make disciples. They were to do that work by going into all the world, baptizing converts into the family of God, and teaching them to obey the commands of Christ. They must do that work because they had been commissioned by the Ultimate Authority who had also promised to go with them, equip them, and give them success.

Those men were well qualified to accept their Commission, because Jesus Christ had made disciples of them. Commissioning them to make disciples of others set the standard and pattern for the work of the Church in the world. Believers in Jesus Christ are first required to be His disciples and then to go and make disciples of others.

Discipling is at the very heart of the work of the Church, and it must be done in accord with the biblical pattern. That biblical pattern is clearly depicted in the life of Simon Peter. He was an exemplary disciple and a model discipler, not only because of the things he did right, but also because of the things he did wrong. Fallen sinners learn best from those who teach by their words and by their examples both how to obey and how to repent.

A Little Help From a Friend

Peter's example in Scripture encourages us to walk in his footprints because it is so realistic. When the Holy Spirit inspired the writers of Scripture to tell us so much about Peter, they painted an accurate picture that has helped a myriad of saints down through the ages.

When we look at Peter, we see a man who was sometimes clear-sighted and sometimes confused, sometimes appealing and sometimes exasperating, sometimes quite humble and sometimes quite arrogant, sometimes courageous and sometimes fainthearted. We see a man who loved the Lord deeply and was committed to serving Him well. But we also see a man who was immature in His faith and thus often in trouble. We see a man who, although very weak, was also chosen of God, beloved by God's Son, and indwelt by God's Holy Spirit. In short, we see a man who was a great deal like us. We can identify with him, and that helps us learn from him.

Peter walked down the same kinds of roads that we're called to walk. He climbed the same kinds of hills, reclined in the same kinds of green pastures, detoured around the same kinds of roadblocks, fell into the same kinds of potholes, and arrived safely in heaven. Peter's example makes an excellent road map for those whom Christ has called to be His disciples. Patterning our lives after the fisherman's can help us walk worthy of our high calling in Christ.

The writers of Scripture gave us a realistic picture of Peter (and of many other saints also) both to encourage us and to warn us as we serve our Lord Jesus. Peter was a great disciple of Christ, but he was also a great sinner. And the presence of sin in his life consistently drove him to the foot of the Cross. Peter's obvious, undeniable flaws — and his response to them — remind us of our total dependence upon God's enablement as we work out our salvation.

Peter's example encourages us by affirming that the presence of sin in our lives doesn't mean we aren't Christians, nor does it invalidate our witness for Christ. Although it is true that modern-day Christianity is far too undemanding of its adherents, we must not fall into the snare of expecting perfection of ourselves or others. One of the most effective means of proclaiming God's grace in our dying culture is acknowledging sin and seeking forgiveness through earnest repentance.

Our highly tolerant, psychologised culture no longer accepts the biblical concept of sin. "Sin," as defined in God's Word, has been redefined by society in terms of mistakes, failures, dysfunction, maladjustment, co-dependence, victimization, poor self-esteem, or faulty socialization. On those rare occasions when we do hear the word "sin" bravely (or snidely) bandied about, its context is usually our relationships with each other instead of our fallen condition before a holy and righteous God.

Better testimony to others to HUMBLE ourselves :

Although you and I grieve over this state of affairs, we should be quick to see an opportunity here. Our own sins provide us with a platform to teach, by our example, a biblical concept of sin and to display the glory of God's gracious forgiveness. Those who know us well should see and hear us confessing our sin for what it really is — transgression of God's commands. They should see us repenting for the right reason — because our behavior is offensive to God. And they should see us honor Him with our thanksgiving and joy when we receive His gracious, cleansing forgiveness. Our families, our neighbors, and our friends and associates should understand the biblical concept of sin (even if they refuse to accept it) because they have seen it lived out in our daily activities.

We sin AGAinst God, not others

No 'But's' - you caused me to sin (justify)

Peter's example also encourages us by reminding us that we *grow* in grace. Growth, by definition, is an ongoing process, not an instantaneous occurrence. As we follow Peter through the Gospels and on into Acts, we see a man who is growing in grace. When we read his epistles, we see a man who has grown even more. He did not attain perfection in this world, but as he walked with the Lord, he became wiser, stronger, and more self-controlled. How did he do it? By putting aside sinful behavior and longing for the pure milk of the Word. His own words proclaim that this is the way that God's children grow in respect to salvation (1 Peter 2:1-2). Watching him grow encourages us as we grow. It also encourages us to be patient with others as they grow. The oft-heard reminder, "God isn't finished with me yet," although trite, is still true.

Peter's example in Scripture is also a warning to his fellow believers. Although sin should not discourage us in our walk with the Lord, neither should it ever be taken lightly. Sin is always serious and damaging. We should hate it, defend against it, and grieve over it. We should be quick to repent in dust and ashes, and even quicker to mistrust and discount our deceitful hearts. We must never forget that we are *sinners* saved by grace, and that until we are glorified, we will remain highly vulnerable to vicious assaults from the world, the flesh, and the devil. As we seek to serve Christ in our redeemed fallen condition, the wise prayer of the psalmist should be always in mind:

> *Search me, O God, and know my heart;*
> *Try me and know my anxious thoughts;*
> *And see if there be any hurtful way in me,*
> *And lead me in the everlasting way.*
> *(139:23-24)*

I imagine that Peter, the great saint who was also a great sinner, knew his weakness so well that he prayed this prayer constantly.

The Heartbeat of Discipleship

Although Peter was weak, he had great faith in Christ. His great faith had not been dredged up from the depths of his own human weakness; rather, it had come directly from God at the time of his salvation. Great faith always expresses itself in deep love for the Lord and great desire to obey Him. And Peter's great faith was no exception. His often imperfect but completely devoted commitment to Christ reflects the strong, healthy heartbeat of Christian discipleship. Peter's example personifies Jesus' words to His own: "If you love Me, you will obey my commandments" (John 14:15).

Peter's deep love for the Lord motivated the boldness we see in his actions. No cold-hearted man would have stepped out on the stormy waters of Galilee, proclaimed Jesus to be the Incarnate Messiah, or hacked off Malchus' ear with a swiftly-drawn sword. Nor would a cold-hearted man have rebuked the Incarnate Messiah he had just professed, arrogantly over-estimated his own steadfastness, or despaired completely when that overconfidence failed.

Peter's boldness and courage, evident in both his obedience and his sin, sprang from hot, passionate zeal rather than lukewarm indifference. Of course, Peter's passion is no excuse for his sin, but it tells us his heart was in the right place. And when a believer's heart is in the right place, he is highly sensitive to the Holy Spirit's conviction. Peter's great love for the Lord stimulated repentance which gave God an arena in which to display the grace of forgiveness.

Peter's commitment to Christ is a good example for us because it patterns obedience and repentance so well. As we embark on this study and learn to walk in his footprints, my prayer is that *our example* will do the same thing for others.

Review Questions

1. What was the secret of Peter's great influence both during his lifetime and throughout Christian history?

2. Read 1 Corinthians 3:9-17, Ephesians 2:19-22, 1 Timothy 6:17-19, 2 Timothy 2:19, and Revelation 21:14-20. Explain the similarities and differences between worldly support systems and the spiritual support system we have in the foundation comprised of the apostles, prophets, and Christ the cornerstone. Then describe how we should build upon the spiritual foundation God has laid down, and the importance of accepting the responsibility of building upon that foundation.

3. Read Matthew 28:18-20. What is the single command in those verses (the imperative verb)? What are the three instructions supporting that single command (the participles)? What two motivations does Jesus add that encourage us to obey the command by following the instructions in these verses? Explain Jesus' marching orders for His Church in your own words. According to Jesus, what is *your* responsibility as a member of His Church? List some ways you may fulfill this responsibility in your own sphere of influence.

4. Describe several ways that Peter's example has helped Christians down through the centuries carry out Christ's Great Commission. Be sure to include both the encouragements and the warnings we find in his example.

5. How does great faith express itself? Can you think of some specific ways in which Peter's great faith expressed itself in his life?

Applying the Word

1. This week begin memorizing one or more of the following verses:
   Psalm 139:23-24
   Matthew 28:18-20
   John 14:15

2. Read 1 Corinthians 3:9-17 and 15:58. Use a dictionary if necessary to help you define the words "steadfast," "immovable," "abounding," "toil," and "vain." Now spend some time thinking about a typical week in your life. Are your routine daily activities, attitudes, and thoughts characteristic of someone who is steadfast, immovable, and always abounding in the work of the Lord? Explain, citing specific examples. Review the lesson material and explain how the example of Peter's obedience and sinfulness might help you gain assurance that your toil is not in vain in the Lord. (Hint: Think about what prompted Peter's obedience and how he responded to his sins.)

Digging Deeper

1. Read Jesus' marching orders to His Church recorded in Matthew 28:18-20, paying particular attention to His use of the words "all" and "always" in those verses. Spend some time studying and meditating on Jesus' words and then explain the significance of the following phrases:

a. "*All* authority has been given to Me in heaven and on earth."

b. "make disciples of *all* nations"

c. "teaching them to observe *all* that I commanded you"

d. "I am with you *always*"

Then explain how Jesus defines discipleship in these verses. What activities are you currently pursuing that will enhance your effectiveness as a disciple of Christ? What activities are you currently pursuing that will hinder your effectiveness as a disciple of Christ? What changes do you need to make in your activities? Make a specific step-by-step plan to begin making those changes. (Be sure that your plan answers the questions: Who?, What?, When?, Where?, and How?.)

*"It was out of love for the world
that God revealed eternal truth to the world."*

❧

F. F. Bruce

Chapter 2

Simon Peter, Meet the Master

(*Bible reading: John 1:1-51; 6:37-40; 17:1-26; Ephesians 1:3-14; Titus 1:1-3*)

"Simon, we have found the Messiah!"

I can't help but wonder what flashed through Simon's mind when his brother Andrew delivered this bombshell. Was it something like, *Hallelujah! Bless you for telling me. Let's drop everything and become His disciples.* Or was it more like, *Oh really? What makes you think this guy is the Messiah?* Or perhaps even something like, *So that's where you've been! Off chasing Messiahs when you should be here, helping me clean these fish.* I have a hunch the last two "hot flashes" are actually closer to Simon's first thoughts than is the first!

The Jews had been looking for their Messiah for centuries and had seen many pretenders rise up and fall hard. Simon Peter had every reason to be downright skeptical of his brother's enthusiasm. But Andrew must have had some credibility and influence with cynical Simon because he finally convinced him to come and meet Jesus of Nazareth.

I wonder if Peter tried to talk some sense into Andrew before he agreed to go with him. I wonder if he tried to persuade him that the "real Messiah" was more likely to announce His arrival at the Jerusalem Temple than in the region of Galilee. I wonder if he finally agreed to meet Jesus so that he could expose Him as yet another pretender and put an end to this nonsense once and for all. Maybe then Andrew would spend more time with the nets and less time hanging around that strange desert prophet.

I also wonder what flashed through Simon's mind when he actually came face to face with Andrew's Messiah. I wonder what thoughts and emotions seized him the first time Jesus' eyes locked on his and looked straight into his soul. I wonder if Simon realized in a heartbeat that Jesus had known him long before he was born — had, in fact, known him since before time began.

All According to Plan

Long ages ago, before time began, the triune Godhead lived in eternity. God the Father, God the Son, and God the Holy Spirit had always lived and would always live in perfect relationship with one another. The Godhead was not lonely and did not need anything. The Three of Them could have continued eternally in that Divine Status Quo...but we know that They didn't. They chose instead to create, and the world in which you and I live is the result.

Most of us wonder from time to time why God freely chose to create a realm comprised of heaven and earth, fill it with beings able to disobey Him, and permit them to fall into rebellion and sin. Since we know that the God who created all things is holy, righteous, and good, we scratch our heads when we ponder the state of His world. If He is all-powerful, how did His perfect Creation end up such a mess?

The answers to questions like these can't be found in the rocky shallows of creaturely reasoning. Rather, they must be painstakingly dredged up from the depths of God's revelation. The prophecy of Isaiah is a good place to start. There we read that God's ways are not our ways and His thoughts are not our thoughts (55:8-9). We must adjust our thinking to His if we want true understanding of the things He has done. We must understand that He is God, and there is no one like Him (46:9). And we must realize that He determined the outcome of all things before anything happened, and that He controls every circumstance to accomplish His purpose (v. 10).

The current condition of our fallen world doesn't shock God. He isn't worried about the way things are going. He never wonders if His plan will work out the way He intended. Instead, He flatly asserts through the mouth of His prophet, Isaiah, "Truly I have spoken: truly I will bring it to pass. I have planned it, surely I will do it" (v. 11). God's world doesn't look nearly as messy to Him as it does to us. That's because He is the Designer, and we are but small parts of His design. Since His perspective is infinitely broader than ours, we are wise not to lean on our own understanding, but to trust Him wholeheartedly as we look at His actions through the lens of His Word.

The End For Which God Created the World

Why did the eternal God create a world? Why did He choose to create beings who could, in turn, choose disobedience? And why did He allow His perfect creation to fall prey to sin? The Bible tells us He did all those things to display His own glory. Does that surprise you? Perhaps even shock you? Does the fall of mankind into sin seem antithetical to displaying God's glory? It did to me too until Jonathan Edwards showed me the connection.

In his great classic, *The End for Which God Created the World*, Edwards describes God's creative actions in terms of an "overflow" or "bubbling over" of His glorious attributes.[1] In other words, God was *not* so lonely all by Himself in eternity past that He created some company. God was *not* lonely in His perfect triune relationship with the Son and the Spirit. And He did *not* have needs only creation could meet. Rather, creation occurred a "natural result" of His glorious attributes. Edwards compares those attributes to a full fountain whose natural tendency is to overflow. In a very real sense, God could not "contain" His own glory. His attributes demanded display. And creation displays them.

In the opening verses of Psalm 19, Israel's King David proclaims:

> *The heavens are telling of the glory of God;*
> *And their expanse is declaring the work of His*
>   *hands.*
> *Day to day pours forth speech,*
> *And night to night reveals knowledge.*
> *There is no speech, nor are there words;*

Their voice is not heard.
Their line has gone out through all the earth,
And their utterances to the end of the world.
In them He has placed a tent for the sun,
Which is as a bridegroom coming out of his
  chamber;
It rejoices as a strong man to run his course.
Its rising is from one end of the heavens,
And its circuit to the other end of them;
And there is nothing hidden from its heat.
(vv. 1-6)

The Apostle Paul reminded the Christians at Rome that God's eternal power and divine nature are clearly seen in His work of creation and leaves those who deny Him without excuse for their foolishness (1:20). However, God's glorious attributes also overflow His work of creation. Although His marvelous Universe says a lot about God, it does not say it all. It cannot speak of His love, mercy, and grace, nor of His justice and wrath. And it only hints at the fact that He is thrice holy, righteous, and good. *Those glorious attributes are only fully displayed in God's work of redeeming a number of His fallen creatures from the power of sin.*

The prophet Isaiah declares that God redeems sinners for the purpose of displaying His glory:

> *But now, thus says the* LORD, *your Creator, O*
>   *Jacob,*
> *And He who formed you, O Israel,*
> *"Do not fear, for I have redeemed you;*
> *I have called you by name; you are Mine!...*
> *For I am the* LORD *your God, The Holy One of*
>   *Israel, your Savior...*

Since you are precious in My sight,
Since you are honored and I love you...
Do not fear, for I am with you;
I will bring your offspring from the east,
And gather you from the west.
I will say to the north, 'Give them up!'
And to the south, 'Do not hold them back.'
Bring My sons from afar,
And my daughters from the ends of the earth,
Everyone who is called by My name,
And whom I have created for My glory,
Whom I have formed, even whom I have made.''
(43:1, 3-7)

Paul also affirms that redemption's chief end is the glory of God in the opening verses of the book of Ephesians. In 1:3-14, he details the work of each Person of the Godhead in the redemption of sinners, and declares that Each does His work for the praise of God's glory. Moreover, Isaiah and Paul don't stand alone in these statements. From beginning to end, God's Word associates His great plan of redemption with the *full* display of His glory.

God's Love Gift to His Son

Just as God did not create because He needed some company, He did not save sinners because He needed to love them. Scripture is clear that God *is* love, and that His love was completely expressed and requited within the confines of the Godhead (See 1 John 4:8; John 3:35, 5:20; 10:17; 15:9; 17:24, 26). God loves, not out of need, but out of nature. Therefore, the salvation of sinners was not only a means of displaying His glory, it was also a means of expressing His love.

If you grew up in church, you are no doubt aware that God's gift of salvation was motivated by His great love for His chosen children. But you may not be aware that His love for His chosen children was what Jonathan Edwards referred to as a *subordinate motive*. A subordinate motive, as its name implies, is one that derives from and is necessary to fulfill a *chief motive*.[2]

For example, if I want to become a medical missionary, I must first study the Bible and complete medical school. Becoming a medical missionary is my chief motive. Studying the Bible and completing medical school are subordinate motives that derive from my chief motive and are necessary to accomplish it. I will not achieve my chief motive if I fail to achieve the subordinate ones; however, I may also fail to achieve my chief motive if I allow the subordinate ones to overshadow it. If I lose sight of my chief end, I am likely to spend my whole life in school and never set foot on the mission field!

That's why we need to remember that God's love for us is subordinate to His love for His Son. God bestows upon us the great gift of salvation so that He can give Jesus Christ the far greater gift of a redeemed people who will serve and glorify Him forever. Thus, the love motivating the salvation of sinners is *chiefly* God's love for His Son and *subordinately* His love for fallen sinners. Our salvation is a means by which God expresses His love for His Son.

Paul alludes to this fact several times in his letters. In Titus 1:1-2, he says that the knowledge of the truth which is according to godliness, in the hope of eternal life "was promised *before times eternal*." Obviously, that promise was made *to the Son* because we did not yet exist. In 2 Timothy 1:9, Paul affirms that we were chosen "in Christ Jesus *from all eternity.*" And in Ephesians 1:4, he says again that we were chosen in Christ *"before the foundation of the world,* that we should be holy and blameless before Him."

Jesus spoke of the love gift God had given Him when He told His disciples: "All that the Father gives Me shall come to Me, and the one who comes to Me I will certainly not cast out....And this is the will of Him who sent Me, that of all that He has given Me I lose nothing, but raise it up on the last day" (John 6:37, 39). And He referred to it again in His High Priestly Prayer: "Father, I desire that they, also, whom Thou has given Me, be with Me where I am, in order that they may behold My glory, which Thou hast given Me; for Thou didst love Me before the foundation of the world" (John 17:24).

The salvation of sinners occurred because, in eternity past, the Father, motivated by His love for the Son, promised Him a gift of a people for His own possession. The Son, motivated by love for the Father, agreed to pay the full price of redeeming those people. And the Holy Spirit, out of love for Them both, took on the role of Agent in that great work. This was the eternal Covenant of Redemption which guarantees the salvation of those God has chosen for inclusion in His gift to His Son. And if you are a part of that gift, you are truly blest!

The Role of the Gift

The fisherman brothers, Andrew and Simon, were part of the love gift God promised His Son. So were all of the faithful Old Testament saints. So were all those who believed on Jesus Christ while He walked this earth. And so are all those who have come to know Him during the two millennia hence. When Andrew and Peter met Jesus, they probably sensed that He had known them long before they had met Him. But I'm sure it took them awhile to understand the role they were expected to play as part of God's gift to His Son.

The role of a gift is to bring joy to its recipient, not to manipulate that recipient into fulfilling all its felt needs. A gift is at the disposal of the one to whom it is given to use as he or she chooses. It is unwise and unseemly for a gift to put its own desires ahead of the one who receives it. A gift that behaved in this way would most likely be reprimanded severely, both by the giver and by the recipient.

Although we know very little of how Andrew understood and fulfilled his role as a gift, we know quite a bit about Simon. As we study the ways in which He related to Christ, we will see that he did not always behave in a manner befitting God's love gift to His Son. In fact, we don't see *consistent* love-gift-like conduct from Peter until we move out of the Gospels and into Acts.

But Jesus was always patient with Simon. You see, He had known from before time began what this rugged fisherman would become in His service. I'm sure that when Jesus first laid eyes on Simon, He looked right past his rough edges and saw rock-solid Peter — the man upon whom He would build His church in the world. What a moment that was! "You are Simon the son of John; you shall be called Peter," Jesus said, indicating to all within earshot that God's grace would work wonders with this particular man. What a blessing to know that God's grace works the same kind of wonders with you and me. If you are a Christian, you and I are also a part of God's gift to His Son. Jesus has known since before time began what each of us will become in His service.

Of course, Jesus knew that Simon Peter had a long way to go. Just like everyone else in God's gift, Simon was definitely a "fixer-upper"— but Jesus had come to earth for the very purpose of fixing. As we map the progress of Simon Peter's relationship with Jesus Christ, we'll see how Jesus worked on him and in him until He could use him. And we can rejoice in the knowledge that He works on and in us for the very same purpose.

Notes:

1. For an excellent introduction to Jonathan Edwards and a little help in reading this great classic treatment of God's chief end in creation, see John Piper, *God's Passion for His Glory: Living the Vision of Jonathan Edwards*. Wheaton, Ill.: Crossway Books, 1998.

2. For more information on this subject of chief and subordinate ends, see John Piper's book referenced above.

Review Questions

1. Read carefully and thoughtfully: John 1:1-51; 6:37-40; 17:1-26; Ephesians 1:3-14; Titus 1:1-3. What evidence do you find in those verses to support the assertion that Jesus knew Peter long before Peter met Jesus? How long had Jesus known Peter? Which verses tell you this? What do these verses tell you about the nature of salvation?

2. Read carefully and thoughtfully: Isaiah 43:1-13, 45:20 - 46:13; 48:11; 55:1-11. What truths do you find in these verses that help you understand why God created beings with the ability to disobey Him? What truths do you find that help you understand why He allowed those beings to fall into rebellion and sin?

3. Explain in your own words the similarity between God's acts of creation/redemption and the "behavior" of a full fountain. How do Psalm 19 and Isaiah 43 support this analogy?

4. What was God's chief motive in saving sinners? What was one of His subordinate motives? How are these two motives related? How do Titus 1:1-3, 2 Timothy 1:9, Ephesians 1:4, John 6:37-40, and John 17:24 reveal these motives?

5. What is God's love gift to His Son? How did each member of the Trinity participate in the giving of this gift? How does understanding salvation in terms of God's love gift to the Son influence your assurance and confidence in your relationship with the Lord?

6. Describe the role of a gift. What do we all need to play our role effectively?

Applying the Word

1. This week review the verse(s) you began memorizing last week. Then begin memorizing one or more of the following:
   Isaiah 46:9-10
   Isaiah 55:8-9
   John 6:37-40

2. Review and ponder the Scripture passages from this chapter that reveal redemption to be both a display of God's glory and an expression of His love. Does careful consideration of these verses change your understanding of salvation? If so, how? If you are a Christian, describe what being a part of God's love gift to His Son means to you personally. Is your conduct (thoughts, attitudes, and behavior) appropriate for one who is part of this gift? Cite specific examples of conduct which is appropriate and conduct which is not. Make a step by step plan to strengthen appropriate conduct and to mortify that which is inappropriate. If you are not a Christian, read Appendix A, and ask God to help you understand how you can become a part of His love gift to His Son.

Digging Deeper

1. Read John Piper's book, *God's Passion for His Glory: Living the Vision of Jonathan Edwards*. Use what you learn from this book to formulate an answer to the question, "Why did God create the world?" Express this answer in your own words and in three different versions — a short version (one minute or less), a medium version (approximately 15 minutes), and a long version (approximately 30 minutes). List people within your sphere of influence who need to know why God created the world. When and where might you use each of your answers to minister to each of those people?

*"If the kingdom of God has come near,
and the King himself is already present,
life must change."*

~

Sinclair B. Ferguson

Chapter 3

From Fisher of Fish to Fisher of Men

(Bible reading: Exodus 3:1-12; Isaiah 6:1-8; Matthew 4:12-25; Mark 1:14-20; Luke 4:14-5:11)

I imagine that Simon was tired and frustrated that day. He and his brother had been fishing all night but had nothing to show for it. Simon was, almost assuredly, *not* looking forward to cleaning and mending his unfruitful nets, although he knew there was no way around that discouraging task.

As he neared the shore, he probably noticed the crowd. His mood may have lightened a bit as he nudged Andrew and said, "Looks like Jesus is here." I imagine that Simon was happy about that. Listening to Jesus would take his mind off last night and speed up the task of cleaning and mending those unfruitful nets.

Simon and Andrew had been "following" the new Rabbi named Jesus for almost a year.[1] That is, they were following His teaching without following Him physically. Their families and jobs kept them in Capernaum while Jesus traveled through Galilee and taught in the synagogues.

Rumor had it that He had been well-received in the region — except in His home town of Nazareth. There He had claimed to be the fulfillment of Isaiah's prophecy and had almost been killed. Somehow He had escaped from a murderous mob, but no one was quite sure exactly how He had done it.

Amazing things had been happening right in Capernaum. Jesus taught *with authority* both in the synagogue and in the streets, something the people were not accustomed to hearing. He rebuked and cast out diseases and demons, demonstrating that His authority went well beyond words. The sick and possessed were being brought to him in droves, and all of them left completely healed and in their right minds.

Simon might not have believed it if he hadn't seen it with His own eyes. His mother-in-law had been one of those Jesus had healed. She had become very ill and was suffering with a frighteningly high fever when the family asked Jesus to help her. Jesus had simply entered the house, stood over the sick woman, and rebuked the fever. Instantly, she had become well, strong, and eager to serve them.

Simon may have been thinking of that day at his house as he climbed out of his boat and began washing his nets well within earshot of the popular Teacher. He may have noticed the crowd growing larger and pressing around Jesus, and quickly complied when Jesus commandeered his boat to use as a "pulpit." They put out a little way from the land where Jesus sat down to finish His teaching. Then Jesus did an unusual thing. He turned from the crowd and told Simon to head for deep water and let down his nets.

I can almost hear Simon thinking, *Are you out of your mind? We've been out there all night, and they're just not biting. All I want to do is get these nets cleaned and go home to bed.* But to his credit, he didn't say what he was thinking. My guess is that Simon was struggling to reconcile his own professional knowledge of fishing with the miraculous things he had seen Jesus do. Professionally, he knew that deep water was no place to fish in broad daylight...and yet, neither are diseases and demons cast out by mere words. Obviously, Simon's amazed regard for this Rabbi overruled his own instincts. "Master," he said. "We worked hard all night and caught nothing, but at Your bidding I will let down the nets."

As soon as he did, he got the shock of his life. Every fish in the lake jumped into those nets! The nets started to break, and Simon frantically called to his colleagues to come to his aid. Both boats were soon so full of fish that they started to sink. It took only a moment for Simon to realize the significance of what he was witnessing. Jesus was not a professional fisherman; He was the Creator of fish, and fish obeyed His commands. In a flash, Simon knew he was standing in the holy presence of God.

Interestingly, Simon was not the least bit inclined to pound the Lord on the back, give Him a thumbs-up, and proclaim, "Way to go, God!" Such behavior was the farthest thing from his mind. As a devout Jew, Simon knew he was a sinner and that sinners cannot survive in the holy presence of God. In sheer terror, he crumpled to the deck of the boat and cried out, "Depart from me, for I am a sinful man, O Lord!"

Simon may well have expected to die on that deck. But he didn't. The holy presence of God in which he was cringing did not consume him, although it could have. Jesus Christ — God Incarnate and Simon's Messiah — transformed him instead.

Transformed to Serve

Simon's reaction closely resembled those of other saints who had suddenly encountered the holy presence of God. In Exodus 3, a fugitive prince by the name of Moses turned aside to investigate a strange bush that was burning but not being consumed. As he approached, a voice exploded out of the bush and commanded him to remove his sandals because he was standing on holy ground. "I am the God of your father, the God of Abraham, the God of Isaac, and the God of Jacob," the voice proclaimed. Scripture informs us that Moses was frightened and "hid his face, for he was afraid to look at God."

And in Isaiah 6, the prophet saw the Lord sitting on a lofty, exalted throne with the train of His robe filling the Temple. Six-winged angels (seraphim) were standing above the throne and calling out to each other, "Holy, Holy, Holy is the LORD of hosts, the whole earth is full of His glory." As they spoke, the foundations of the Temple shook and the room filled with smoke. Isaiah was terrified. The glory of God's majestic holiness had illumined his own wretched sinfulness, and Isaiah disintegrated. "Woe is me," he cried out, "for I am undone! Because I am a man of unclean lips, And I dwell in the midst of a people of unclean lips; For my eyes have seen the King, the LORD of hosts." (NKJV)

Obviously, suddenly finding oneself in the holy presence of God is *not* a comfortable, relaxing experience. None of these men were the least bit inclined to run into God's arms or curl up in His lap and snuggle a while. I get the impression they all wanted to run, but were too frightened to move, much like a deer on the highway standing frozen in the glare of oncoming headlights.

What was it that caused robust, hardy men to react this way? The answer is simple. Each one had seen God's holiness light up his own sinfulness. And each of them seemed to understand at that moment that God is too holy to look on evil and wickedness. They knew that God's holiness and their sinfulness could not exist in the same space, and that whenever they end up in the same space, holiness wins.

However, holiness doesn't necessarily win by destroying the sinner; sometimes it wins by transforming the sinner. R. C. Sproul explains that "there are two ways to fear God. Both involve trembling at His greatness, but they run in opposite directions. One sort of fear is mixed with hatred, so that we flee from God, but certainly without love in our hearts. But there is also the fear that is mixed with love, so that we shyly and tremblingly seek to draw near to him despite his great majesty."[2]

Moses, Isaiah, and Peter were terrified by their experiences and probably wanted to run. But their love for God compelled them to run toward Him instead of away from Him. They drew near in fear and were greatly blessed by God's transforming power. Moses, the fugitive prince who was slow of speech and slow of tongue, was equipped and commissioned to face the same Pharaoh who had set the price on his head and to demand the release of God's covenant people. Moses returned to Egypt a much different man from the one who had fled.

Isaiah was not left to cower on the floor of the Temple. God dispatched one of His angels with a hot coal from the altar to purge the sin from the prophet's lips. "Behold this has touched your lips; and your iniquity is taken away, and your sin is forgiven." The sin that could not exist in the presence of God had been removed from Isaiah as far as the east is from the west. He had been forgiven and was clean in God's sight. Holiness had won by separating the sinner from the guilt of his sin. But that's not all. Isaiah was also transformed from a cowering sinner to a humble servant.

When God said, "Whom shall I send, and who will go for Us?", Isaiah responded without hesitation, "Here am I. Send me!" He didn't ask God for a job description, salary potential, and benefit summary before committing himself. He had no idea what he was getting himself into, but he had every confidence in the One who was getting him into it. God's majestic holiness, which was undeniably fearsome, was also completely trustworthy. Isaiah walked out of the Temple a much different man from the one who had entered.

The radical life-change we see in Moses and Isaiah also took place in Simon the fisherman. His close encounter with God did not destroy him; it transformed him instead. Simon's cry from the deck reflected repentance; and Jesus' response assured him of forgiveness and cleansing. "Do not fear, from now on you will be catching men." His sin had been removed from him and was out of God's sight. He had been accepted in the Beloved and commissioned for service. From that day forward, Simon would catch men for God's kingdom instead of fish for the market. He walked away from his boat a much different man from the one who had launched it.

A Closer Look

At this point, we would be wise to pause and ponder three critical aspects of Simon's encounter with Jesus: (1) The clear manifestation of Jesus' glorious Lordship, (2) the startling response evoked by it, and (3) the abrupt change of lifestyle that it produced.

Jesus displayed His sovereign Lordship over Simon's whole life by taking control of his *business* as well as his religion. Jesus' miracle brought Simon the fisherman face to face with the infinite power of God Incarnate over *all realms of life*. Simon could not deny that the holy presence of God had put those fish in his nets; and he could not escape the deep sense of sin and distress evoked by God's holy presence.

Simon's response to Jesus' manifestation of Lordship over all of his life was one of *repentance and confession*. Think about that for a moment. Does it strike you as strange? Why didn't Simon, the sharp businessman, whip out a contract and sign Jesus on as part of his crew? After all, with Jesus "on board," he could look forward to fabulous wealth and early retirement! Many in the evangelical church today seem to respond in that way to the pervasive power of the Lord Jesus Christ. They want to get Him "on board" so they can use His great power to further their own worldly purposes.

A.W. Tozer described this attitude well when he said, "Left to ourselves we tend immediately to reduce God to manageable terms. We want to get Him where we can use Him, or at least know where He is when we need Him. We want a God we can in some measure control."[3] However, when Simon recognized God in his boat, he didn't respond in that way. As the hymn writer so aptly put it, the things of earth had grown strangely dim in the light of God's glory and grace. The idea of using Jesus' power for his own ends was the farthest thing from Simon's mind. His thoughts were consumed with *conviction* as he gazed on the holiness displayed in that power.

Simon saw his fallen sinfulness illumined dramatically against the shining backdrop of Jesus' majestic holiness. Simon knew at that moment that he was offensive to God and had no right to survive in His holy presence. But instead of collecting the wages of sin, he received the unmerited favor of God in the grace of repentance. His soul-shattering confession reveals God's mercy at work in the heart of His chosen sinner. Simon now understood, with crystal clarity, the message he had heard preached by John the Baptist and Jesus: "Repent, for the kingdom of heaven is at hand!" The King was now standing in his fishing boat, extending to him the indescribable gift of forgiveness and cleansing.

Simon arose from the deck a changed man. Jesus had called him and his colleagues to pursue a new focus. From now on they would fish for men instead of for fish. Jesus had no doubts about how they would respond. The impelling force of His influence over the hearts and minds of these men reflected His greatness, not theirs. He had revealed Himself to them as God in their boat; He had displayed His sovereign Lordship over the whole of their lives; He had called them to pursue His kingdom and righteousness. Their response was inevitable. Luke tells us "when they had brought their boats to land, they left everything and followed Him" (5:11).

Trust Me, I'm God

Simon Peter is known for his impetuosity. However, his decision to leave everything and follow Jesus was most definitely *not* an impetuous action. Rather, it was a reflection of implicit trust. Much like his predecessor, Isaiah, Simon had no idea what he was getting himself into, but he trusted the One who was getting him into it. The holy presence of God in his boat was just as trustworthy as it was fearsome.

Simon's commitment to Jesus wasn't bound up in a bevy of "if, then" stipulations. He didn't condition his service on guaranteed outcomes. When Simon left everything on the shore of the lake, he didn't know how he was going to make a living...he didn't know how he was going to provide for his family...he didn't know if he would be in danger...he didn't know if he would be effective. *But he knew Jesus*. And that's all that mattered.

His mind was set on the things above instead of the things on the earth, and he was willing to risk any and all temporal loss for the enduring blessing of eternal gain. Simon had taken the first step required of those Jesus calls to be His disciples. He had forsaken the world, turned away from reliance on his own understanding, and placed his trust in his Lord. For the rest of his life, Simon would walk very closely with Jesus. And although his future steps often faltered, they never turned back.

I find myself convicted by Simon's example. I am one of those queasy Christians who avoids risks at all cost. I want all my bases covered before I step out to serve God. If there's a chance I could get hurt, lose money, offend my loved ones, or generate some hostility, then I tend to question the wisdom of pursuing that ministry. I find it hard to trust God when I don't have a clue how things will turn out. I want guarantees. Simon has helped me to see that I need to change if I am to respond to Christ's call to discipleship. I don't *need* guarantees; I *need* to trust Jesus. That's the faithful response to the One who gave me salvation. The power revealed through His holiness that conquered my sin can also conquer my fears.

How about you? Have you been convicted by Simon's example? If so, consider what kinds of changes you need to make in your thoughts, attitudes, and behavior as you work through the questions that follow.

Notes:

1. Most commentators agree that the events recorded in John 1:19-4:42 occurred during the interval of about a year between Jesus' baptism and the beginning of His Galilean ministry.

2. R. C. Sproul, *Before the Face of God, Book 3: A Daily Guide for Living from the Old Testament* (Grand Rapids, Mich.: Ligonier Ministries and Baker Books, 1994), 442-443.

3. A. W. Tozer, *The Knowledge of the Holy* (San Francisco: Harper and Rowe, 1961), 8.

Review Questions

1. Read carefully Matthew 4:12-25, Mark 1:14-20, and Luke 4:14-44. (If you have time, read also John 1:19-4:45.) Then describe in your own words Jesus' relationship with His disciples during the first year or so of His public ministry. You may speculate a bit, but be sure to tie your speculations to Scripture. Include in your description the events that occurred in Capernaum, and explain how these events may have influenced Simon.

2. Read carefully Exodus 3:1-12, Isaiah 6:1-8, and Luke 5:1-11. Explain Simon's unusual reaction to Jesus after the huge catch of fish. How is his reaction similar to that of Moses and Isaiah when they encountered God? Explain the significance of the similarity between these three men's reactions.

3. Describe the *transformations* experienced by Moses, Isaiah, and Simon Peter. For what purpose were these men transformed?

4. How did Jesus manifest His Lordship over all aspects of Simon's life? How did Simon respond? Explain the significance of his response.

5. How did Simon's life change dramatically as a result of his encounter with Jesus? Does his example convict you? If so, explain.

Applying the Word

1. This week review the verses you have memorized from previous lessons. Then begin memorizing one or more of the following:
       Isaiah 6:1-4
       Matthew 6:33-34
       Colossians 3:1-2

2. John Piper defines a risk-taker as one who "performs an action that exposes him to the uncertain possibility of injury or loss." (*The Pleasures of God: Meditations on God's Delight in Being God* [Sisters, Ore.: Multnomah Publishers, 2000], 57) Thus, risk always involves uncertainty about the outcome of a particular action. Based upon this definition and verses such as Isaiah 46:9-10, we know that God *never* takes risks. Since He has declared "the end from the beginning," He is never in doubt about the outcome of any action. Christians, however, do take risks in God's service because they don't know the future. Following Christ as His disciple could therefore be described as a "risky" endeavor. What are some specific "risks" that you take in following Christ? Describe both the action involved and the possible outcomes. Do you hesitate to obey Christ in certain areas because of the risks involved? If so, explain. How might the knowledge that God does not take any risks stimulate you to take a few more risks in His service? Explain your answer thoroughly. How will taking more "risks" in God's service give Him greater glory? How will it enhance your joy in His service?

Digging Deeper

1. Read either *The Holiness of God* by R.C. Sproul or *The Knowledge of the Holy* by A. W. Tozer. Based upon what you learn from your reading, prepare an outline that will help you explain the relationship between understanding God's holiness and pursuing effective discipleship. How might you use this outline to help those within your sphere of influence understand this important relationship?

"[Peter] is always wading into water too deep for him, yet always turning back to his Master like a little child."

❧

Edward Donnelly

Chapter 4

Risky Business

*(Bible reading: 2 Samuel 10:6-14; Esther 3:7-4:16;
Matthew 14:13-33; Mark 6:30-52; Luke 9:10-17; John 6:1-71)*

Simon quite naturally assumed a leadership role within the group of twelve men who had "left all" to follow Jesus. In every biblical list of these men, his name appears first, and he often spoke for the group when Jesus asked them a question. Such a turn of events shouldn't surprise us at all. God had chosen this man before time began to be instrumental in building His church. He had designed Simon fearfully and wonderfully to accomplish the work prepared for him to do. He had honed Simon's God-given leadership skills in the earthly occupation of fishing, and introduced him to Jesus at just the right moment. When Simon became a fisher of men, he was the right man for the job of leading the Rabbi's band of disciples. He was the one they could count on to "boldly go" into uncharted territory and blaze a trail they could tread with assurance.

Simon took risks (and a great deal of heat) in the service of Christ; however, the risks that he took (and the heat that he bore) mirrored his dependence on Christ. That is what made him an exceptional leader. Simon had recognized Jesus as God Incarnate; and he knew that God, the omniscient Lord of the Universe, *never* takes risks. Therefore, he could trust Jesus implicitly when Kingdom service looked like risky business to him.

When he couldn't see past his first step into uncharted territory, he knew that God knew the end from the beginning and would accomplish His purposes. I think Simon may have often encouraged the other disciples with words very similar to those of Charles Spurgeon: "Never let us fear that our consecrated stores will not hold out, or that we have not talent or ability enough if the Lord is pleased to use us."[1] Simon's boldness was fueled by his unflagging confidence in God's sovereign power.

Who Are All These People, and Why Do They Want to Be My Disciples?

True disciples of Christ are willing risk-takers, but they are not foolish risk-takers. They obey God's commands in the face of the "uncertain possibility of injury or loss"[2] because of their trust in God's sovereign power. They understand Esther's decision to "go in to the king, which is not according to the law; *and if I perish, I perish*" (Esther 4:16). And they know exactly why Joab told Abishai before a great battle, "Be strong, and let us show ourselves courageous for the sake of our people and for the cities of our God; and may the Lord do what is good *in His sight*" (2 Samuel 10:12). Esther went in to the king *without knowing* whether she would survive the encounter. Joab *didn't know* on the eve of battle whether his forces would defeat the Arameans. Both were facing the uncertain possibility of injury or loss — and both obeyed God despite their uncertainty.

Esther and Joab were most clearly risk-takers, but they were most clearly *not* foolish risk-takers. Taking risks in obedience to God's commands is *invariably* wise, because such risks are taken in pursuit of His kingdom and righteousness. Foolish risks are those taken in pursuit of human agendas. God has declared through the prophet Isaiah that His purposes will be established, that He will accomplish all His good pleasure, and that He will surely do all He has planned (46:10-11). When disciples of Christ take risks in pursuit of His kingdom, they do so with assurance that the God-ordained outcome will further His purposes.

Taking wise risks is what distinguishes real disciples from false ones. Hoards of people followed Jesus all around Galilee — an action that certainly entailed some risk. Not only were they were neglecting their homes and businesses, but they were also inciting the wrath of their political leaders. The spectacular result of the disciples' first "training mission" had reached Herod's ears, and he was upset. Jesus, knowing the time for confrontation had not yet arrived, withdrew with the Twelve to a "lonely place" for a time of refreshment.

The multitudes followed persistently — and foolishly. Scripture says the majority of them were pursuing Him for their own human purposes instead of for God's. They were willing to risk neglecting their homes and their businesses because they had seen Him work miracles. And they were willing to risk Herod's wrath because they planned to make Jesus their king. Of course, Jesus knew that most in the crowd were not real disciples. And He chose to act on this occasion to distinguish the true from the false.

He began by performing one of His most spectacular miracles — feeding more than 5000[3] people by continually multiplying five barley loaves and two tiny fish. Everyone ate to full satisfaction and left plenty to feed the Twelve and their Lord. The miracle had its desired effect. The crowd's passionate, self-centered desire to take Jesus by force and make Him their king became clearly evident; and Jesus responded by separating Himself and the Twelve from the reach of their greed. He sent the Twelve across the Lake to Bethsaida, then dismissed the clamoring crowd, and went up on the mountain to pray. Having physically separated the true from the false, He would proceed to confirm the status of each.

Real Disciples Walk on Water

I'm sure that Jesus put Simon in charge of the men in the boat, and I'm equally sure that Simon did not want to go. My hunch is he wanted to stay and help Jesus "straighten out" the misguided crowd on the shore. Nevertheless, Simon obeyed his Lord — and soon found himself in incredible danger.

Night was falling when they set sail, and before they had gone very far a fierce storm hit them full force. Simon was quite familiar with Galilee's storms and knew for a fact that their lives were in danger. As he pulled on the oars and tried to keep the others from panicking, he may well have questioned the wisdom of his obedience!

The terrified men in the boat battled the storm almost all night. Scripture tells us it wasn't until the fourth watch of the night (between 3AM and 6AM) that Jesus came to their rescue. Why the delay? Was He so engrossed in His prayers that He didn't know that they needed Him? Did He know they were in trouble, but didn't think He could help them? Was He upset with them and getting some satisfaction from letting them suffer? Did He figure that they were expendable, and that if they didn't make it to shore, He could easily recruit a dozen more men? Of course not!

Because Jesus was so engrossed in His prayers, He knew they were in trouble. He also knew that He could *and would* help them at precisely the moment that would serve God's purposes best. If Jesus had been upset with them, He would have rebuked them on shore for their benefit — rather than leave them to suffer for His satisfaction. And He did not consider these men to be expendable, replaceable assets. He knew that God had specifically chosen them before time began to be the foundation of His Church in the world.

Simon may have been wondering about the wisdom of obedience, but Jesus knew that His men were perfectly safe in God's care. John MacArthur has said, "When believers are in the place of obedience they are in the place of safety, no matter what the circumstances. The place of security is not the place of favorable circumstances, but the place of obedience to God's will....Faith is strengthened by its being taken to extremities it has never faced before."[4] The risk of discipleship had resulted in danger, but the omnipotent Governor of all earthly circumstances would accomplish His purposes. And part of His purpose in this circumstance was strengthening the faith of the men in the boat.

After struggling all night against the storm and their fear, those men were surely close to exhaustion. Naturally, when they saw what looked like a man walking toward them *on the water*, they cried out in terror, "It is a ghost!" You know, of course, that it wasn't a ghost, but their Lord and Savior, who immediately calmed them by saying, "Take courage, it is I; do not be afraid."

I find the wording of that statement to be highly significant. Jesus exhorts them to "take courage" in their recognition of Him. *Then* he tells them, "do not be afraid." I think He is implying that courage is drawn from reliance on Him, and that fearlessness results from such courageous reliance. Simply telling someone not to fear is rarely effective unless we also give them a good reason not to. Jesus' good reason for them not to fear was that He was there. Their circumstances had not changed; the storm was still raging. But their Master was present. Recognizing His nearness infused them with courage in the midst of their circumstances and allayed their fears.

Simon, their leader, seemed completely unable to contain his excitement. In a typical burst of enthusiasm, he refused to wait patiently for Jesus to get to the boat, but called out to Him over the raging storm, "Lord, if it is You, command me to come to You on the water." I can almost see Jesus smiling as He called back to the fisherman, "Come!"

I wonder if the other men in the boat were watching in horror as Simon lowered himself into the waves. I wonder if they were all holding their breath as they watched him take one courageously reliant step after another on top of the water. I wonder if their hearts all missed a few beats when he paused, looked around, and suddenly sank out of sight! How frightened they must have been when he cried out in panic, "Lord, save me!" And how huge must have been their collective sigh of relief when Jesus stretched out His hand and pulled their soaked leader out of the drink. I wonder if they heard Jesus say to him, "O you of little faith, why did you doubt?"

I don't think Jesus was angry with Simon. I think He was delighted that Simon was out there with Him. I think Jesus loves it when His children trust Him enough to boldly go into uncharted territory — when their reliance upon Him gives them the courage to take risks for His sake. I think He understands when they get distracted by frightening circumstances, take their eyes off of Him, and sink out of sight. And *I know* that He never takes His eyes off of them when they are in trouble. He protects them even when they allow their own doubts to inundate faithful behavior. And the moment they call out for help, He lifts them up and reminds them that their faith needs to be strengthened. His gentle rebuke also serves as encouragement to beef up their faith with ongoing exercise.

I think the men in that boat learned a lot from their leader that night. I think they learned that courage for service comes from keeping their eyes on the Lord, that shifting their eyes to their circumstances replaces courage with weakness, and that seeking help from the Lord always overcomes weakness. I think God orchestrated their circumstances that night to teach them those lessons, and I think He used Simon's enthusiasm to make sure that they learned them. God knew that those men would face many more storms in the future and that weathering them would require courageous reliance on Jesus.

Real Disciples Don't Run With the Crowd

The Twelve may have thought that their troubles were over as soon as Jesus stepped into the boat and the storm suddenly stopped. In thankful relief, they worshipped Him, saying, "You are certainly God's Son!" (Matthew 14:32-33). However, more trouble was heading toward them on shore.

The crafty crowds had been investigating the mysterious disappearance of Jesus and soon discovered Him on the other side of the sea. "Rabbi, when did You get here?" They asked, perhaps eager to hear the details of another miracle. Jesus declined to answer their question, but addressed their spiritual condition instead. The twelve true disciples, fresh from their brush with physical death, listened as Jesus explained the grave spiritual danger inherent in the crowd's purely physical focus. They were more interested in food for their bodies than they were in food for their souls. And until they developed a taste for spiritual bread, the physical bread that they wanted wouldn't do them much good.

Physical bread would sustain their lives temporarily, but only spiritual bread could give them life everlasting. Jesus told them quite bluntly that *He* was that life-giving spiritual bread, and that unless they were willing to "eat the flesh of the Son of Man and drink His blood," they would have no life in themselves (John 6:53). "My flesh is true food, and My blood is true drink." Jesus said. "He who eats My flesh and drinks My blood abides in Me, and I in him. As the living

Father sent Me and I live because of the Father, so he who eats Me, he also shall live because of Me" (vv. 55-57).

Those words were shocking to Jewish ears. The Law strictly forbade the consumption of blood, and the very idea of "munching" on human flesh was abominable. The crowd was now grumbling about Jesus' difficult saying and wondering aloud, "Who can listen to it?" To this Jesus responded forthrightly, "It is the Spirit who gives life; the flesh profits nothing; the words that I have spoken to you are spirit and life" (vv. 60, 63).

Eternal life is given by God through the work of His Holy Spirit. A hunger and thirst for spiritual sustenance is given to those whom the Father has chosen to give to His Son. All those the Father has given the Son will come to Him, driven there by their hunger and thirst for the spiritual food He provides. All those who come to Him, He will receive, because He knows that no one will come except those drawn by the Father (vv. 37, 44). Those who aren't drawn to Him by the Father will find His saying too difficult and refuse to hear it.

Jesus knew that very few in the crowd on that day were seeking Him because of their spiritual hunger and thirst. Surely, His tone was somber and serious when He dismissed those who were not with these words: "But there are some of you who do not believe....For this reason I have said to you, that no one can come to Me, unless it has been granted him from the Father" (vv. 64-65). A true disciple named John who heard those words fall from his Lord's lips on that day, tells us that many withdrew and walked no more with Him (v. 66). Jesus had clearly succeeded in separating true disciples from false. The silence must have been deafening when Jesus turned toward the Twelve who were still standing with Him. "You do not want to go away also, do you?"

He knew the answer to that question, of course. And so did they. But they needed to voice it to confirm their commitment. As usual, their bold leader, Simon, spoke for them all. "Lord, to whom shall we go? You have the words of eternal life. And we have believed and have come to know that You are the Holy One of God" (vv. 68-69). I imagine that Jesus looked into the eyes of each man in that group to seal each one's commitment. He knew that one would be His betrayer but that even that one had been purposely chosen. God had given Him the remaining eleven to serve as the foundation for His church in the world. They had come to Him seeking fulfillment of their spiritual hunger and thirst, and they would not be denied. They knew that He called them to the risky pursuit of His kingdom, and they had accepted that call in courageous reliance upon Him.

I imagine that Jesus' eyes rested finally on those of Simon. And I don't think Simon blinked. This man would be their leader, both now and after Jesus was gone. He would not lead perfectly, but he would lead well. He would teach them about courage, and he would teach them about failure. He would teach them to follow, and he would teach them to repent. He would learn from His Lord and teach others what he had learned. Simon was without doubt a true disciple, and he would make true disciples of others.

Notes:

1. Charles Haddon Spurgeon, *The Gospel of Matthew*, gen. ed. Larry Richards (Grand Rapids, Mich.: Fleming H. Revell, 1987), 194.

2. John Piper, *The Pleasures of God: Meditations on God's Delight in Being God* (Sisters, Ore.: Multnomah Publishers, 2000), 57.

3. Scripture tells us that Jesus fed 5000 *men* that day, and most commentators assume there were also women and children in the crowd. The "guestiments" of how large the crowd actually was range from around 6000 to well over 20,000. Regardless of the number you settle on, this is still a spectacular miracle.

4. John MacArthur Jr., *The MacArthur New Testament Commentary: Matthew 8-15* (Chicago: Moody Press, 1987), 442-3.

Review Questions

1. What motivated Simon's willingness to take risks in the service of Christ? Read Esther 3:7-4:16 and 2 Samuel 10:6-14. Describe the risks taken by Esther and Joab in these situations. Were Simon, Esther, and Joab foolish or wise in their willingness to take these risks? Explain your answer. Now consider the risks taken by the large crowds that followed Jesus all around Galilee. Were the majority of these people acting wisely or foolishly? Explain your answer.

2. Read John 6:1-71. How did Jesus unmask false disciples in this series of events? How did He confirm the genuineness of His true disciples?

3. How "safe" were the Twelve in the midst of the storm on the Sea of Galilee? Does being "safe" in God's service mean that obedient disciples will never be injured or killed? Explain your answer.

4. Explain the significance of Jesus' words to the terrified men in the boat fighting the storm on the Sea of Galilee.

5. Was Simon's exuberant request to come to Jesus on the water foolhardy? Why or why not? What enabled him to walk on the water? What caused him to sink? What saved him from drowning? What lessons did the men in the boat learn from Simon that night?

6. Read John 6:22-65 and summarize the main points of Jesus' teaching in these verses (commonly known as the Bread of Life Discourse). Describe the effect of His teaching on the hungry crowds. Describe the effect of His teaching on the Twelve. How do you account for the difference in their reactions?

Applying the Word

1. This week review the verses you have memorized from previous lessons. Then begin memorizing one or more of the following:
    Psalm 5:11
    John 6:68-69
    2 Corinthians 9:8

2. Reread Matthew 14:13-33 and your answer to Review Question #5. The *principle* taught in this passage of Scripture is *not* that all Christians should literally walk on water in the middle of storms, but that we should look to Jesus for strength to do what He calls us to do. He often calls us to tasks that are both risky and beyond our ability so that He will be glorified in our obedience. List one or more things you believe He has called you to do that are either risky or beyond your ability. Describe your response to His call. (Have you sought strength from Him to do these things? Or, have you declined to heed His call, citing all kinds of "good reasons" why you can't possibly do what He wants you to do? Did you begin in reliance on Him and then "sink out of sight" because of fear or distraction? Are you still floundering? If not, how did you recover?) Describe one or more ways that Simon's example encourages you to pursue God's kingdom and righteousness even when such pursuit is risky or beyond your ability.

Digging Deeper

1. Consult reliable Bible study aids, including good commentaries, in consideration of John 6. Then explain in your own words why John 6:37 in no way contradicts John 6:44 and John 6:65. Discuss your conclusions with your pastor, an elder of your church, or another of your church leaders.

*"Let us never fall into the trap of thinking that
because we are sure of one thing,
we are therefore sure of everything."*

J. Glyn Owen

Chapter 5

From Foundation Stone to Stumbling Block

(Bible reading: Matthew 16:13-28; Mark 8:22-38; Luke 9:18-27; 1 Corinthians 10:12; Galatians 2:20; Ephesians 2:19-22)

Unlike redemption, discipleship is a process. When God redeems us from the power of sin, He transfers us *instantaneously* from the kingdom of darkness into the kingdom of light. Then He begins to develop us as disciples through a *process* of growth. We come into God's family as ignorant babes who must grow in the knowledge of our Lord Jesus Christ if we are to fulfill God's purposes for us.

Jesus illustrated this truth for His twelve disciples when He healed a blind man *progressively* near the Galilean city of Bethsaida. Some townspeople begged Jesus to heal the man, and Jesus complied — but in a strange manner. He led the man outside of the city, away from the crowds. There His disciples watched Him spit on the man's eyes, lay His hands on him and ask, "Do you see anything?" The man looked up and said, "I see men, for I am seeing them like trees, walking about." Jesus then laid His hands on the man's eyes, and his sight was fully restored (Mark 8:22-26).

Simon may well have been watching and thinking, *Man, what a tough case. Even Jesus had to go at it twice.* It's quite likely that Simon and his eleven companions missed the point of the miracle at the time Jesus performed it, but it wouldn't be long before they would get it. Jesus withdrew with them to the northern villages of Caesarea Philippi where He asked them, "Who do people say that I am?"

The disciples reported all the popular scuttlebutt. Some say, John the Baptist, back from the dead. Some say, Elijah, or Jeremiah, or one of the prophets. Jesus probably paused and looked right into their eyes. He then asked them the most significant question they would ever consider. "But who do you say that I am?"

Without hesitation, Simon responded, "Thou art the Christ, the Son of the living God." I think if we'd been there, we could have heard a ripe fig drop as Simon's words hung in the dry desert air. Simon himself may have been surprised by the profundity of what had just fallen out of his mouth. He had actually declared that, contrary to local opinion, the Rabbi from Nazareth was much more than one of God's prophets — even much more than one of God's prophets back from the dead. He was, in fact, the Messiah...the Deliverer...the Mediator...the One sent from God the Father in the power of His Spirit to be the ultimate Prophet, Priest, and King of His people. He was the unique Son of God, the sole source of life.

Where did Simon's surprising, profound declaration come from? Certainly not from popular scuttlebutt or local opinion. Jesus said, "Blessed are you, Simon Barjona, because flesh and blood did not reveal this to you, but My Father who is in heaven." The words that had fallen from Simon's mouth came as a result of God's direct revelation. Those words were extraordinary — the last thing he would have been "programmed" to say by his Jewish upbringing. They did not reflect the established beliefs of his generation concerning the Messiah, nor did they reflect the traditional teachings of Jewish leaders. Simon said what he said by divine inspiration.

Interestingly, this revelation of critical truth hadn't come quickly to Simon. He had been walking with Jesus for close to three years, and during that time he had been growing progressively. Until this startling moment, however, his perception of Jesus had been rather blurry — much like the "trees walking about" perceived by the blind man Jesus had healed. But God chose this moment to clear up his vision. By blessing him with the favor of divine inspiration, God sharpened his sight to see Jesus distinctly.

With the keen eyes of faith, Simon saw Jesus as the Father's ambassador, sent with authority to declare God's mind, unveil His heart, and disclose His will. Simon saw Jesus as One commissioned by God to make peace with those He had chosen for life everlasting. And he saw Jesus as Lord, the One to whose rule he would gladly submit and to whose purposes he would sincerely commit the rest of his days.

This was a turning point in Jesus' relationship with His disciples. Almost three years of teaching, exhorting, encouraging, and praying had culminated in God's revelation of the Son's true identity. Most scholars believe that Simon spoke for the group, not just for himself, when he responded to Jesus' watershed question. Since none of the others spoke up to contradict or correct his profound declaration, it appears that the Twelve were in perfect agreement. Their sure recognition of Jesus as Christ sealed their dedication to loyal discipleship. Although they were still sinful men and would continue to struggle with weakness and confusion, they were wholly committed to following Jesus as their Lord Christ, the Messiah.

Simon Becomes Peter, the Foundation Stone

Jesus went on to tell Simon that day: "And I also say to you that you are Peter, and upon this rock I will build My church; and the gates of Hades shall not overpower it. I will give you the keys of the kingdom of heaven; and whatever you shall bind on earth shall be bound in heaven, and whatever you shall loose on earth shall be loosed in heaven" (Matthew 16:18-19).

I wonder if Simon's mind flashed back immediately to the words Jesus had spoken to him on the day they had met: "You are Simon the son of John; you shall be called Cephas" (John 1:42). "Cephas" is translated "Peter," and it means *stone*. Jesus had recognized Simon the fisherman as Peter the stone at the moment that Andrew had first introduced them. But He knew it would take time for Simon the fisherman to grow into Peter the stone. Jesus had patiently cultivated this precious disciple for almost three years — equipping and preparing him for this decisive moment. Having seen and declared God's revelation about who Jesus was, Simon was now ready to hear God's revelation about who he himself was.

Simon the fisherman had become Peter the stone — the rock upon which Jesus Christ would build His church in the world. That rock would provide such a solid foundation that the gates of Hades would be unable to overpower Christ's church. Peter would hold the keys of the kingdom, binding and loosing on earth those things which had already been bound and loosed by God in heaven.[1]

Theologians have argued down through the ages about whether the "rock" upon which Christ built His Church was Peter the man or Peter's confession. Perhaps I am engaging in oversimplification, but I like to think that Christ built His Church on *Peter the Confessor*. I hold that opinion for two primary reasons: (1) I don't see how we can legitimately separate Peter the man from Peter's confession, and (2) Ephesians 2:20 teaches that Christ's church is built on the foundation of men[2] — the inspired apostles and prophets, among whom Simon Peter was highly significant.

Peter's confession of faith in Jesus Christ was not something separate or set apart from Peter the man; rather it was a clear reflection of who Peter the man had become. He had experienced salvation and was a new creation in Christ. He had been transformed by Jesus' work of redemption. His old self had been crucified and no longer lived. Peter's confession was evidence that he now lived by faith in the One who had loved him and delivered Himself up for him.

The Peter who said, "Thou art the Christ, the Son of the living God" was a product of grace. And for that reason alone he would be useful to God. Before time began, God had ordained Peter's salvation by grace and had prepared certain good works for him to do. Included among those good works was the task of church building. William Hendriksen comments that during the early history of the Church, Peter was the most powerful and effective human link between Jesus and His church as well as the most influential means of its inward and outward growth[3] Most commentators agree that Mark, whose Gospel was a primary source for both Matthew and Luke, was in effect, "Peter's interpreter." And Peter's own epistles beautifully articulate the eternal value of Christ's life and death.

Surely, Christ did build His church upon the rock of Peter confessing his faith by God's gracious enablement. Peter was a significant part of the foundation of apostles and prophets upon whom the Church stands, but he was in no way superior to any of them. Peter was called as a leader who would represent the apostles, but there is no evidence in Scripture that he was infallible.

When Jesus gave Peter "the keys of the kingdom," He gave them to Peter the leader, not to Peter exclusively. Scripture reveals that all the apostles made use of these keys, which opened and closed the doors of God's kingdom through preaching the Gospel and exercising church discipline.[4] By submitting themselves to the teachings of Jesus, they "bound" and "loosed" on earth what had been bound and loosed in heaven.

Binding and loosing has to do with permitting and forbidding, and the word "whatever" indicates that this binding and loosing refers to things such as beliefs and practices. Although binding and loosing does not refer to people explicitly, it does have clear implications regarding the standing of church members. The keys of the kingdom are still used by ordained church leaders today, but not in the same way they were used by the Apostles. The Apostles were often guided in their use of the keys by direct revelation, whereas church leaders today are guided solely by God's written word.

God builds His kingdom by building His Church, and since He will accomplish all His good pleasure, His church is invincible. God identifies Himself with His people, the Church, and will preserve them through all manner of difficulty and trial. But that doesn't mean we can simply sit back and enjoy the ride. We are responsible to seek His Kingdom first by living our lives with God-centered perspectives. When we allow our minds to shift focus from the things above to the things of the world, we quickly stumble and fall in our pursuit of God's kingdom. Peter the leader learned this lesson the hard way, and his example warns those of us who think we are standing to take heed lest we fall.

Peter the Stone Becomes a Stumbling Block

Jesus had waited until late in his ministry to teach His disciples about His death on the cross. He was The Master Teacher, of course, who taught progressively as well as repetitively. He knew that before these twelve men could comprehend the need for His death, they had to be firmly grounded in the truth of His identity. After Peter's confession, He knew it was time to prepare them for the impending Cross.

Matthew says "from that time, Jesus Christ began to show His disciples that He must go to Jerusalem, and suffer many things from the elders and chief priests and scribes, and be killed, and be raised up on the third day" (16:21). Peter, no doubt euphoric in his new position of "foundation stone," responded in pride and quickly became a huge stumbling block. He took Jesus aside and proceeded to rebuke Him by saying, "God forbid it, Lord! This shall never happen to You" (v. 22).

I have no doubts that Peter's brash words poured out of a heart filled to the brim with good intentions. I'm sure he loved Jesus wholeheartedly and desired above all things to protect Him from harm. I'm sure he believed he was responsibly building Christ's church by doing whatever was needed to save the life of her Head. I'm sure he would have laid down his own life in a heartbeat in defense of his Messiah. But I'm also sure that Peter was looking at this situation from his own worldly perspective instead of from God's.

Scripture emphasizes how easily we fallen sinners (even we *redeemed* fallen sinners) misconstrue God's intents and purposes (often with good intentions) when we view circumstances through the lens of our humanness instead of the lens of His Word. Isaiah proclaims that God's ways are not our ways and His thoughts are not our thoughts. God's thoughts and ways are *higher* than ours and thus take in more territory. Because God has ordained the end from the beginning, He knows how each circumstance fits into the accomplishment of His eternal decrees. But because our sight is limited in this temporal realm, we need the light of His Word to help us see beyond our immediate circumstances.

Peter's shortsightedness focused his attention on a particular circumstance that seemed catastrophic and in need of averting. Rather than seek an eternal prospective from Jesus, he jumped right into trying to fix it himself. Fortunately, he didn't get very far. You see, Jesus loved Peter (and the rest of His Church) enough to stop him dead in his tracks by rebuking him in return. "Get behind Me, Satan! You are a stumbling block to Me; for you are not setting your mind on God's interests, but man's."

How shocking those words must have been to Peter! How could Jesus have looked at him and seen Satan so soon after seeing the *rock* upon which His church would be built? Of course, Jesus knew that Satan attacks most effectively when Christians are glowing in triumph from a fresh spiritual victory. Peter's overconfident "high" gave Satan an opening to tempt both Peter and Jesus to short-circuit God's plan of redemption by bypassing the Cross.

Jesus had seen that temptation before — in the wilderness immediately after His baptism. He recognized in Peter's words one more satanic attempt to persuade Him to seize the crown without enduring the Cross. He knew that Peter was being used by the devil and did not understand the full implications of what he was saying. Peter could not have realized at that time that circumventing the Cross would have prevented salvation, nor could he have known that winning that argument would have cost him his soul. Peter did not yet understand the absolute need for the Atonement; therefore, he did not perceive that the way which seemed right to him at that moment would have ultimately been the way of death.

Jesus knew that the "Rock" upon whom His church would be built needed more teaching before he could accomplish the good work prepared for him before time began. And His shocking words were as much a protection of Peter as they were a rebuke to the devil. They served as sharp, much needed instruction that shortsighted human perspectives are downright destructive in church building endeavors.

Jesus went on to tell Peter and the other eleven disciples that those who wish to come after Him must deny themselves, take up their crosses, and follow Him. "For whoever wishes to save his life shall lose it; but whoever loses his life for My sake shall find it. For what will a man be profited, if he gains the whole world, and forfeits his soul? Or what will a man give in exchange for his soul?" (vv. 25-27). Discipleship demands an eternal perspective. Every thought, word, attitude, and action must be considered in light of its effect on the soul. Shortsighted, earthbound perspectives foster absorption with self-centered interests instead of the interests of God. Those who would follow Jesus must crucify self and seek His Kingdom first.

Peter had grown a great deal in his three years with Jesus, but he still had a lot of growing to do. In the months leading up to the Cross, Peter would take many giant steps forward and also fall a few giant steps backward, but overall he would grow in God's grace and in the likeness of his Lord Jesus Christ. And as we saw in this lesson, his successes *and* failures have been recorded in Scripture to help Christians down through the ages walk in his footprints and grow in the same ways that he did. Before going on to the exercises, please pause for a moment and pray for God's help in applying the lessons of Peter's example in order to walk in a manner worthy of your high calling in Christ.

Notes:

1. The verbs translated "shall be bound" and "shall be loosed" are perfect passive participles which refer to action completed in the past with continuing results into the future. Many Bible scholars indicate that the clearest translation of these verbs is "will have been bound" and "will have been loosed."

2. Bear in mind that the cornerstone of that foundation of men is Jesus Christ, and that without that precious cornerstone, the foundation of men would be very shaky indeed.

3. William Hendriksen, *New Testament Commentary: Matthew* (Grand Rapid, Mich.: Baker Book House, 1973), 648.

4. See Questions 83-86 of the Heidelberg Catechism with Scripture texts.

Review Questions

1. Reread Mark 8:22-30. Then explain in your own words how the miracle Jesus performed in these verses illustrates the progressive nature of discipleship. In what ways might this miracle have prepared the disciples for the events that would soon occur in Caesarea Philippi?

2. Explain the significance of Simon's statement, "Thou art the Christ, the Son of the living God." Be sure to include the significance of the statement's source as well as its meaning.

3. In what way(s) was Simon's statement about Jesus a turning point for the whole group of disciples?

4. Do you think Christ built His church on Peter the man, on Peter's confession, or on Peter the confessor? Explain your answer supporting your ideas with Scripture references.

5. What are the "keys of the kingdom"? How did the first century Apostles use these keys differently than they are used by church leaders today?

6. Describe how Peter went from foundation stone to stumbling block. Include a description of the temptation behind his well-intentioned words to Jesus.

7. Was it necessary for Jesus to rebuke Peter so severely? Why or why not? Explain how Jesus' words were protection for Peter as well as rebuke. Then explain how Jesus' words about cross-bearing added correction to rebuke and thus helped Peter grow.

Applying the Word

1. This week review the verses you have memorized from previous lessons. Then begin memorizing one or more of the following:
   Matthew 16:24-26 or Mark 8:34-37
   Galatians 2:20
   1 Corinthians 10:12

2. Describe one or more principles of Christian growth you learned from this lesson. Include in your description how Peter exemplified that (those) principles. How does Peter's example *convict* you regarding your own Christian growth? How does his example *encourage* you in your Christian growth? Give one or more specific examples of how your growth in Christlikeness is similar or different from Peter's. What are some practical ways in which you might use what you have learned in this lesson to help other people become more effective disciples?

3. Read Matthew 4:1-11 and Luke 4:1-13. Explain how Satan tempted Jesus in these verses to seize the crown without enduring the Cross. Note in Luke 4:13 that Satan departed from Jesus "until an opportune time." Do these words help you understand the significance of Peter's rebuke of Jesus and of Jesus' severe response to Peter? If so, explain. How do these verses underscore the importance of doing God's work in the way God has prescribed? Describe one or more ways you have been tempted to do God's work by ungodly means. Do you need to repent and confess any specific sins of "short-circuiting" God's means and methods? If so, take some time and do that now.

4. Taking up our crosses to follow Jesus has to do with crucifying self-interest rather than bearing with difficult circumstances or people. In what specific ways do you need to crucify self-interest in order to become a more effective disciple? List one or more self-centered thoughts, attitudes, or activities about which God has convicted you. (If you can't think of any, try pride.) What do you need to do in order to crucify these specific self-centered thoughts, attitudes, or activities? When will you begin to do these things? Who will you ask to hold you accountable? If you are accustomed to thinking of difficult circumstances or people as "crosses," how should you begin working to change your thinking in this area? In light of God's sovereign ordaining of the circumstances of your life, how should you think of difficult circumstances or people?

Digging Deeper

1. William Hendriksen states in his commentary on Matthew that the very best commentary on Matthew 16:24 is Galatians 2:20. Read these two verses carefully and explain whether you agree or disagree with Dr. Hendriksen.

*"In the Christian theology of history,
the death of Christ is the central point of history.
Here all the roads of the past converge.
Hence all the roads of the future diverge."*

Stephen Neil

Chapter 6

Converging to Diverge

---

*(Bible reading: Matthew 17:1-8; Mark 9:2-8; Luke 9:28-36;
John 1:14; Philippians 2:5-8; 2 Peter 1:16-19)*

The week[1] following Peter's landmark confession at
Caesarea Philippi must have been difficult for him. Although
Jesus had honored him with the position of "foundation
stone" of His Church, He had also rebuked him severely
for acting as he thought a foundation stone should. Jesus
had said that Peter was setting his mind on man's interests
instead of on God's, and that anyone wanting to follow
Him must be willing to take up his cross and die for His
sake. There was no profit, He said, in gaining the world
and losing your soul.

I'm sure Jesus' words were unsettling for Peter. His
upbringing in Judaism had not prepared him to follow the
Messiah *to death*. He was expecting the One sent by God
to overthrow Roman rule and establish the Kingdom on
earth. Wouldn't that be, in a sense, "gaining the world"?

Had not Jesus said He was "going to come in the glory of His Father with His angels; and will then recompense every man according to his deeds"? Hadn't He also promised that some of the disciples would actually see Him "coming in His kingdom" before they died? How could those promises be kept if Jesus were killed in Jerusalem? If Jesus were the Messiah, why would the leaders of Judaism put Him to death? And if they succeeded in killing Him, wouldn't all the souls of God's people be lost forever?

Peter must have agonized greatly over questions like these during the days that followed his Lord's baffling rebuke. I wonder if Peter discussed his perplexity with the other disciples. Or if he took his confusion to Jesus and sought clarification. Or if he withdrew into silence and pondered alone. We have no way of knowing because the Gospels don't tell us. But we can be sure that, in any case, Jesus knew Peter was struggling — and that He allowed him to struggle to strengthen his faith — and that He refused to allow Peter's struggle to tempt him beyond what he could bear.

The Ultimate "Mountain Top Experience"

Six days after Jesus rebuked the foundation stone of His church, He took Peter, James, and John up on a mountain to pray. These three men were the core of His band of disciples and would bear the heaviest weight in leading His Church. Peter would be their outspoken leader; James would be their first martyr; John would outlive them all and see visions beyond his own time and place. Two of them would be responsible for writing much of the New Testament, and one of them would set the standard for self-denying discipleship.

These three were in need of particular preparation that would equip them to lead leaders with fearless assurance. The "mountain top experience" that they shared on that day would undergird their commitment to Jesus Christ, their Messiah, and leave lasting impressions on their future service. However, when the three set out for the mountain with Jesus, none seemed to sense that this "prayer retreat" with the Lord would be so momentous. Luke tells us that while Jesus was praying, they sank into slumber.

Their fatigue may have been due to discouragement or depression over Jesus' insistence upon the need for His death. They no doubt found it almost impossible to jettison firmly ingrained notions about the Kingdom of God. They may have been wondering if Jesus really was the Messiah since His plans seemed so out of line with Jewish interpretations of scriptural prophecy. Had they "forsaken all" to follow the wrong man, after all?

Of course, they had not. And God was about to convince them of that in a startling manner. When they awoke, they saw Jesus "transfigured" before them, standing and talking with Moses and Elijah! Jesus did not merely *look different* to them; He *was* different. His whole being had changed substantially so that the glory of deity radiated from every pore in His body. Jesus was not simply reflecting God's glory. The glory of God was pouring from Him.

The Greek word translated "transfigured" is from *metamorpho'ō* which speaks of changing into another form. Although the word is distressingly inadequate to convey the reality of what Peter, James, and John saw on the mountain, it probably comes as close as any single word can. I'm sure that, years later, the gospels writers scratched their heads for awhile as they sought to record this event which not only defies description but explanation as well. John MacArthur says that it was the greatest manifestation so far of Jesus' deity and then comments, "As with the Shekinah manifestation of the Old Testament, God here portrayed Himself to human eyes in a form of light so dazzling and overwhelming that it could barely be withstood."[2]

This revelation of Jesus' deity left an indelible imprint on the three disciples who witnessed it. They had been blessed to see Jesus in His "natural state." They had been blessed with a glimpse of His second coming in glory. They had been blessed with a foretaste of eternity with Him. And they never forgot. The majestic glory of Jesus would be a primary theme of their teaching, preaching, and writing.

The Central Point of History

Of course, the majestic glory of Jesus had been displayed to them for a reason. And that is why Moses and Elijah joined Him on the mountain that day. The three men Jesus had chosen to be leaders of leaders had to know beyond any doubt that He was God in the flesh come to earth to secure their redemption.

You'll remember that before time began, God had chosen a people to give His Son as a gift — a people redeemed from sin's grip to honor and serve Him forever. Redeeming those people required payment of the ransom price set by God — full satisfaction of His holy wrath against sin. It also required perfect submission to His holy Law. None of God's chosen people would be able to redeem themselves because all of them would be "born dead" in their sins. Their redemption depended upon the work of a Substitute.

Jesus Christ committed Himself before time began to be the Substitute for the people God had chosen to give Him. He would give up His right to be equal with God, take on the form of a bondservant, and humble Himself by becoming obedient to the point of death on a cross. He would live as a man on the earth, keeping all God's commandments, and then propitiate[3] God's wrath against the sin of His people. In doing so, He would redeem the elect from the power of sin. His perfect obedience to all of God's Law would be imputed to them as the righteousness needed to enter God's presence; and all of their sin would be imputed to Him in His death, leaving them innocent of sin's damning curse.

God had revealed His holy standard of righteousness in the Law given to Moses, knowing full well that no fallen person would be able to keep it. He did not intend for His Law to be a way of salvation, but a means of highlighting His people's need for salvation. It served as something of a two-sided mirror, reflecting both the perfection of God's standard of righteousness as well as the sinful depravity that prevented His people from conforming to it.

The Old Covenant prophets were faithful to hold the Law's mirror before the face of God's people, reminding them of their sinfulness and of their inability to attain God's perfect standard. Those prophets also reminded the people of God's loving promise to send the Messiah — the perfect Substitute who, in His life and His death, would fulfill the demands of God's Law on their behalf. In His work, and in His work alone, rested the hope of God's people for their salvation. Elijah was one of the boldest of these faithful prophets.

Given this understanding of Old Covenant history, it's no wonder to me that Moses and Elijah were chosen by God to meet with Jesus on the mountain that day. Luke tells us the three of them were discussing Jesus' death in Jerusalem when the disciples awoke (9:31). Apparently, the three groggy disciples easily recognized the two Old Covenant saints and overheard a great deal of their discussion with Jesus.

What they heard testified to the truth of what Jesus had taught them about who He was and why He had come. Their very presence as well as their words said in effect, "This Man is God's Messiah. He is the One we spoke of in the Holy Scriptures. He is the One for whose appearance God's people have been longing for centuries. All of God's Law and all of God's redemptive promises are being fulfilled in Him. In His life, He attained God's perfect standard of righteousness, and in His death, He will satisfy God's righteous wrath against the sin of His people."

The appearance of Moses and Elijah on the mountain with Jesus and His three disciples that day illustrated mostly clearly the *central point* of all human history. All the roads of the past (represented by Moses and Elijah) would soon converge at the Cross. And all the roads of future (represented by Peter, James, and John) would then diverge from there. Jesus, of course, was the focal point of them all. The testimony of God's faithful Old Covenant saints pointed toward Christ's work on the Cross, and the testimony of His faithful New Covenant saints would point back to the same event. Jesus' three key disciples had seen, graphically demonstrated, that God's eternal plan of redemption was centered in the Cross — not in the overthrow of Rome's earthly empire.

A Final Clarification

The lesson could not have been clearer, but Peter seems to have missed the main point. Scholars indicate that the Transfiguration occurred in the month of Tishri (October), during which the Jews celebrated the Feast of Tabernacles. During this feast, the people built and lived in "booths" to commemorate the Exodus from Egypt and the subsequent wandering in the wilderness. Perhaps that explains why Peter blurted out in excitement, "Master, it is good for us to be here; and let us make three tabernacles: one for You, and one for Moses, and one for Elijah" (Luke 9:33).

Peter reacted like most of us do to breathtaking "mountain top experiences." He was more intent upon prolonging the moment than he was on learning and applying the lessons taught by the moment. He wasn't thinking about the significance of how what he had seen fit into the scope of God's eternal plan. He wasn't thinking about his (or anyone else's) need for a Substitute to pay the price for his sin. He wasn't thinking about practical ways to apply what Jesus was trying to teach him. Rather, Peter was wholly consumed with his own excitement. He was so thrilled by what he was seeing that he began making plans to camp out for awhile. But God intervened quickly to clarify his self-centered thinking.

Before Peter's words were fully out of his mouth, the mountain top was enshrouded by an ominous cloud. Fear gripped the men as they heard a voice thunder, "This is My beloved Son, with whom I am well-pleased; listen to Him!" (Matthew 17:5). The men fell on their faces in terror, but

Jesus touched them and said, "Arise and do not be afraid." When they looked up, they saw Jesus alone.

The terror of the Father's startling clarification seared the essential mountain top lesson into their souls. John Calvin described it like this: "God intended that the disciples should be struck with this terror, in order to impress more fully on the hearts the memory of the vision."[4] These three men, who formed the core of Christ's New Covenant Church, would not be allowed to forget, nor to misunderstand, what they had seen. The central point of all human history was the substitutionary death of Jesus Christ, God's Messiah. All Old Covenant roads would converge at the Cross, and all New Covenant roads would diverge from there.

Adjusting Our Focal Points

The three men who witnessed Jesus' transfiguration certainly seem to have had their focal points adjusted to coincide with the Father's. Naturally, their understanding of what they had seen would be deepened as they moved from one side of the Cross to the other, but the lives and words of all three reveal their intense, continuing focus on Christ's work of redemption. The scriptural writings of two of them indicate how great an impact the events on the mountain top had on their thinking.

John opened His Gospel with these stunning words: "In the beginning was the Word, and the Word was with God, and the Word was God....And the Word became flesh and dwelt among us, and we beheld His glory, glory as of the only begotten from the Father, full of grace and truth....For of His fullness we have all received, and grace upon grace. For the Law was given through Moses; grace and truth were realized through Jesus Christ." (John 1:1, 14, 16-17).

And Peter defends his preaching and teaching like this:

> *For we did not follow cleverly devised tales when we made known to you the power and coming of our Lord Jesus Christ, but we were eyewitnesses of His majesty. For when He received honor and glory from God the Father, such an utterance as this was made to Him by the Majestic Glory, "This is My beloved Son with whom I am well-pleased" — and we ourselves heard this utterance made from heaven when we were with Him on the holy mountain. And so we have the prophetic word made more sure, to which you do well to pay attention as to a lamp shining in a dark place, until the day dawns and the morning star arises in your hearts* (2 Peter 1:16-19).

James left no writings in Scripture, but Luke tells us of his willing martyrdom for the sake of the Gospel. The lessons learned on the mountain helped these weak men mature into godly Apostles whose mind and heart focal points had been adjusted to God's. As mature saints, they walked with their eyes fixed on the central point of all human history — the Cross of their Lord and Savior, Jesus the Messiah.

I fear that Christ's Church has allowed her focus to shift away from the Cross in our worldly age. We seem more devoted to comfort and ease than we are to enduring all things for the sake of the chosen. Most of us stumble around in confusion when asked by friendly inquisitors to explain the hope that we have, and we shrivel in fear at the very idea of boldly proclaiming God's truth to those who seem hostile.

Does the Church as a whole need to reset her focus on the central point of all human history? She certainly does! But the Church as a whole is made up of individual Christians. Adjusting the focal point of God's Church requires personal action. As you work through the exercises that follow this lesson, pay close attention to where your focal point is now. If it needs adjusting, ask God to help you fix your eyes on the Cross of your Lord.

Notes:

1. Matthew and Mark indicate that six days elapsed between the Caesarea Philippi confession and the Transfiguration, whereas Luke's gospel says the Transfiguration occurred "some eight days" following Peter's confession. Most scholars reconcile this apparent contradiction by stating that Matthew and Mark counted the days in between the two events while Luke included the days on which the two events occurred in addition to the intervening days.

2. John MacArthur, Jr., *The MacArthur New Testament Commentary: Matthew 16-23* (Chicago, Ill.: Moody Press, 1988), 63.

3. "Propitiation" describes the work of Christ on the Cross that fully satisfied God's wrath against the sin of His elect.

4. William Hendriksen, *New Testament Commentary: Matthew* (Grand Rapids, Mich.: Baker Book House, 1973), 668.

Review Questions

1. Reread Matthew 16:13-17:8, Mark 8:27-9:8, and Luke 9:18-36, paying particular attention to the order of the key events in those passages. Then explain any significance you see in the providential timing of Jesus' Transfiguration in relation to Peter's good confession and subsequent misguided rebuke of Jesus.

2. For what reasons might Jesus have chosen Peter, James, and John to witness His Transfiguration? For what reasons might He have selected *only* those three to witness that particular event?

3. Explain in your own words *how* the Transfiguration manifested the deity of Christ. John MacArthur said that this was the greatest manifestation so far of Jesus' deity. Do you agree with him? Why or why not? Support your answer with Scripture.

4. Describe how the group of men (all six of them) who congregated on the Mountain of Transfiguration illustrate the truth of Stephen Neil's quote that begins Chapter 6.

5. How did Peter react to his breathtaking mountain top experience? How did God's intervention redirect Peter's thinking?

6. Cite some evidence from the "other side of the Cross" that reveals the impact Jesus' Transfiguration had upon Peter, James, and John.

Applying the Word

1. This week review the verses you have memorized from previous lessons. Then begin memorizing one or more of the following:
   John 1:1, 14
   Acts 2:23-24
   Philippians 2:5-11

2. Have you experienced a "mountain top experience" with the Lord? If so, describe it. Did your reaction to this experience resemble that of Peter's? How did God act to help you reset your focus? Describe any lasting impact this experience has had on your life and/or ministry.

3. As a Christian who lives on the New Covenant side of the Cross, how should you contribute to the spread of Christianity throughout the world (on all those diverging roads). Why is it important for you to understand the contribution of those believers who lived on the Old Covenant side of the Cross (those who walked on all those converging roads)? What are some ways you would like to contribute to the spread of Christianity? What do you need to make those desires a reality? Pray about these desires and evaluate which one(s) you should begin to pursue. Then make a specific step-by-step plan that will help you accomplish at least one of your desires to contribute to the spread of Christianity.

Digging Deeper

1. The audible testimony of God's pleasure in His Son at the time of His Transfiguration certainly had a significant impact on Peter, James, and John. Do you think it may also have had a significant impact on Jesus? If so, explain. (The gospel accounts of Jesus' baptism and John 12:20-36 may shed some light on this question.)

"Growth in grace is growth downward;
it is the forming of a lower estimate of ourselves;
it is a deepening realization of our nothingness;
it is a heartfelt recognition that we are not worthy
of the least of God's mercies."

A. W. Pink

Chapter 7

Lessons In Humility

(Bible reading: Matthew 17:22-18:35; Mark 9:33-37, 42-50; Luke 9:46-48, 17:1-4; Romans 13:1-7; Ephesians 4:32; 1 Peter 2:1-17)

People react to extremely bad news in interesting ways. Some "take it like men" with stoic fortitude. Others completely dissolve in grief and despair. Some angrily deny the truth of the news, while others "block out" what they've heard and simply ignore it. Extremely bad news is always a shock to the human psyche and nearly always produces self-protective responses. That's why extremely bad news is best broken gently.

Jesus knew that His disciples would react to the Cross as extremely bad news. He anticipated their shock and was not surprised by their self-protective responses. As God in human flesh, He had expected and fully understood their behavior. But He also recognised the necessity of their coming to terms with His death. The Cross was the central point of redemptive history. Without full atonement for sin, there would be no salvation. The blood of bulls and goats could not take away sin but could only cover it temporarily.

The gift of a redeemed people for His own possession depended upon Christ's perfect sacrifice of Himself on their behalf.

The men Jesus had chosen to lead His New Covenant Church were understandably short-sighted in their view of the Cross. They saw it in terms of their immediate loss instead of as the ultimate gain for all of God's people. They loved and depended on Jesus and did not want to lose Him. They saw the Cross as extremely bad news because they weren't looking beyond their own personal interests. So self-focused and short-sighted were they, in fact, that they appear to have missed altogether Jesus' loving assurances of His resurrection. Their bent toward self-protection temporarily deafened them to the Good News of the Gospel.

Jesus persisted, however, in gently bringing them back to the Cross. Matthew tells us that while they were gathering in Galilee, He said to them *once again*: "The Son of Man is going to be delivered into the hands of men; and they will kill Him, and He will be raised on the third day." And then Matthew says, *once again* they were grieved (vv. 22-23).

What would it take to get through to these men? What would it take to lift their eyes from themselves to God's eternal purpose? What would it take to move them beyond self-protection to complete reliance on their Creator-Sustainer? Actually, it would take quite a lot! But Jesus was willing to do whatever it took. And the first step in the process would be teaching them to be humble.

Who Are the Humble?

The essence of humility is recognition of complete dependence. Perhaps that is why it is considered a virtue by Christians — and a weakness by "humanists." John Calvin said that humility alone exalts God as sovereign. He saw it as an integral part of the abandonment of self-confidence and self-will that constitutes faith.[1]

Faith looks to God's grace instead of human ability. It therefore engenders humility by prompting us to look at ourselves through God's eyes instead of our own. When we see ourselves as we really are — sinful, frail beings of dust, completely dependent on our Creator for every breath, thought, and action — we are humbled and ask with the psalmist, "What is man, that Thou dost take thought of him?" (8:4)

Faith humbles us as we come to appreciate the magnitude of God's grace. We realize that we didn't deserve the great gift of salvation and that even after receiving that gift, we remain embarrassingly unable to do the things He asks of us. Sinful, frail beings of dust cannot merit God's mercy nor satisfy His requirements. Left to ourselves, we can't even demonstrate gratitude in ways that will please Him. Our relationship with Him *depends* on His ongoing expressions of grace toward us. It is by His grace alone that we are saved; and it is by His grace alone that we are equipped for service.

Humility recognizes God's absolute sovereignty. It submits to His purposes because it knows He will fulfill them. It rejoices in the great honor of being part of His means of accomplishing His will. And it delights to obey Him. Humility is therefore essential for those who serve God. The prophet Micah expressed it well, "He has told you,

O man, what is good; and what does the Lord require of you but to do justice, to love kindness, and to walk humbly with your God?" (6:8)

The men Jesus had chosen to lead His New Covenant Church saw the Cross as extremely bad news because they lacked humility. They were not depending on God for right understanding of this distressing event. Nor were they submitting themselves to His purposes, rejoicing to be used in His service, or delighting in obedience. Their example assures us that humility is something that doesn't come naturally. Surely, if they had to learn it, we'll have to also. As we proceed through this lesson, let's pay close attention to what Jesus taught them, and then work hard at applying what we learn to ourselves.

Humility Involves Giving Up Rights

Jesus began with a private object lesson for Peter, the key leader of His band of disciples. Almost immediately upon their return to Capernaum, "those who collected the two-drachma tax" descended on Peter, asking if Jesus was planning to pay. The men probably knew of Jesus' claims to be the Messiah and may have been looking for ways to discredit Him. If He claimed exemption from this particular tax, they would be able to charge Him with irreverence toward God's holy sanctuary. Peter, however, knew that his Master always paid taxes, and assured the collectors that He would pay this one also.

The two-drachma tax was a "temple tax" or "sinner's tax," approved by the Romans for collection by Jewish officials to support the operations of the temple in Jerusalem. Although payment was not legally enforceable, the Jews considered it a moral requirement. The two drachmas (equivalent to a half-shekel) amounted to about two days wages for the average worker. Several months before Passover, collectors fanned out all over Palestine to gather the payments and send them to Jerusalem in time for the annual celebration.

Jesus, of course, had every right to decline paying this tax. The moral responsibility to support the sacrificial system whereby the Jews' relationship with their God was maintained was not incumbent on Him. He was, after all, the Son of the God who demanded those sacrifices. Moreover, He had come to earth in the flesh as both the ultimate Priest and the ultimate sacrifice. His death on the Cross would completely fulfill and thus end the need for an ongoing system of animal sacrifice.

Jesus, however, did not stand on His rights. After explaining to Peter His freedom from obligation in this particular matter, He said, "But lest we give them offense, go to the sea, and throw in a hook, and take the first fish that comes up; and when you open its mouth, you will find a stater [a shekel worth four drachmas]. Take that and give it to them for you and Me" (Matthew 17:27).

This is the only time Scripture tells us that Jesus paid taxes miraculously. And it's probably safe to assume that He didn't have to resort to a miracle this time. I imagine the "money box" kept by the disciples contained enough shekels to cover the payment. However, the use of the miracle reinforced a critical lesson for Peter.

By providing the money from the mouth of a fish, Jesus affirmed His deity while spotlighting the importance of humble submission to God. Demanding His rights would have been unnecessarily offensive to the tax collectors and would have done nothing to further God's eternal purpose. Jesus knew that His Father often worked out His will through human instrumentation, and that therefore seeking God's kingdom *first* often entailed willing submission to human authority.

Peter seems to have learned this lesson quite well. Many years later, he wrote to Christians who were suffering under oppressive regimes: "Keep your behavior excellent among the Gentiles, so that in the thing in which they slander you as evildoers, they may on account of your good deeds, as they observe them, glorify God in the day of visitation....Act as free men, and do not use your freedom as a covering for evil, but use it as bondslaves of God" (1 Peter 2:12, 16).

Humility Involves Becoming Childlike

Peter was not the only disciple who needed to learn a humility lesson. Matthew tells us that while their leader was out fishing for tax money, the other disciples approached Jesus and asked, "Who then is greatest in the kingdom of heaven?" (18:1). Clearly, these men were persisting in self-centered thoughts about the kingdom of heaven instead of humbly submitting their minds to Jesus' teaching. They were not acknowledging their complete dependence upon Him for right understanding, and therefore, missed the whole point of the kingdom of heaven.

Jesus responded graciously to His proud disciples by giving them what they needed (an object lesson) instead of what they deserved (a stern rebuke). He called a little child to Himself and may have pulled him up on to His lap. Then

He revealed the inappropriateness of the disciples' question by explaining that only those who become like little children will enter the kingdom of heaven. Amazingly, those who are as humble as children are the ones who will be the greatest in the kingdom of heaven.

Childlike humility is a prerequisite for receiving Jesus, because children are, above all, dependent beings. They are weak, underdeveloped, immature, vulnerable, unskilled, simple, unpretentious, trusting, and unable to care for themselves. Moreover, they usually recognize their dependence on others and are seldom reluctant to exercise their right of reliance on parents or guardians. Little children are rarely concerned about their own greatness. They focus more on the greatness of the ones who take care of them.

Jesus' self-exalting disciples desperately needed to learn how to be childlike. They needed a reminder that their thoughts were not God's thoughts and that their ways were not His. They needed to remember that He is sovereign over all circumstances of life and that they were not. They needed to recall who they had acknowledged Jesus to be and whose words He spoke. They needed to look to His greatness instead of desiring their own. Being great in the kingdom of heaven results from depending on the greatness of Jesus. And such greatness is reserved solely for those who enter the kingdom through a child-sized door marked "humility."

Humility Involves Concern for Others

As Christ's chosen leaders of His New Covenant church, the disciples also needed a good understanding of how intensely God loves His children. God is the perfect parent and is extremely concerned about the way His children are treated. God identifies Himself with His children, and therefore, takes personally the way people treat them. God told Abraham that He would bless those who blessed him and curse those who cursed him (Genesis 12:3); and the LORD of Hosts assured Zechariah, "he who touches you, touches the apple of His eye" (Zechariah 2:8). Doing good to God's children is pleasing to God, while doing them harm is offensive to Him.

Scripture is clear that God looks out for His kids. And one of the ways that He does that is by giving them leaders. Those who are chosen to lead please God when they follow their Lord's example of humbly serving His people. As Jesus embraced that little child on His lap, He explained to His disciples that the essence of spiritual leadership is deep concern for the welfare of God's precious children.

The disciples had been called and were being equipped to take care of God's kids. And the only way they would be able to walk worthy of that high calling was to acknowledge their complete dependence on Jesus. Deep concern for the welfare of others doesn't come naturally to depraved fallen sinners. It has to be learned. Thus, the first step of their worthy walk was humbly hearing and heeding what Jesus would teach them.

He told them that being deeply concerned about the welfare of God's precious children involves protecting them from harm. Little children are prone to stumble; and when they stumble and fall, they are usually hurt. Because God loves His children, He charges those who take care of them to protect them from stumbling.

Stumbling in Christian service refers to sinning, so what Jesus is saying is that Christian leaders are responsible to protect His children from sin. The writer of Hebrews echoed Jesus' teaching when he admonished believers to "obey your leaders, and submit to them; for they keep watch over your souls, as those who will give an account." He also admonished the leaders to "do this with joy and not with grief, for this would be unprofitable for you" (10:17). We children of God should be very grateful for humble leaders who joyfully bear the burden of watching over our souls. They depend on the Lord to help them spare us the havoc sin can reek in our lives.

God's leaders are charged to protect us from stumbling in various ways. First of all, they must guard against becoming stumbling blocks to us themselves. Leaders who relinquish dependence on Jesus and use their position to pursue personal goals often encourage God's children to sin — either in angry, frustrated response or in gullible acquiescence to God-dishonoring pursuits. Interestingly, Jesus' disciples had actually become stumbling blocks to each other by speculating about who would be the greatest in the kingdom of heaven. Not only were they sinning in their prideful boasting, but they were simultaneously inciting each other to envy, jealousy, and anger.

God's leaders are also required to protect us from stumbling by going in search of stray sheep. Jesus used a brief parable to describe good shepherds as those who leave ninety-nine sheep safe in the fold to go in search of one that is straying. Then He told His disciples, "it is not the will of your Father who is in heaven that one of these little ones perish" (Matthew 18:14). Bear in mind that the "little ones" to whom He referred are those who have come into the

Kingdom through the door of humility. Jesus is talking about Christians who stray away from the safety and protection of His Church, not about lost sinners who haven't yet come to repentance. He is teaching in the context of discipling Christians, not in the context of evangelizing the lost.

Humble leaders sadly acknowledge their sinful tendency to let straying sheep stray. Spiritual search and rescue endeavors are always exhausting and sometimes quite frustrating. It is clearly much easier to focus our efforts on the good sheep in the fold. However, the ones who are straying are God's children too, and spiritual leaders will give an account for their souls as well. There is no way around it; taking good care of God's kids involves going after the wayward.

It also involves correcting those who are sinning. Jesus taught His disciples a process of discipline that would guard God's people against the devastation of sin. Individual Christians would be encouraged to reprove one another in private when sinful behavior was evident. If that action failed to bring repentance about, two or three were to go and confront the sinner together. If that also failed, church leaders must go and admonish the sinner to turn away from his sin and obey God's commands. Those who refuse to repent, even after all this, must be put out of the church to protect other believers.

Jesus concluded His teaching on the importance of deep concern for the welfare of God's children by reminding these leaders, "whatever you shall bind on earth shall be bound in heaven; and whatever you loose on earth shall be loosed in heaven...if two of you agree on earth about anything that they may ask, it shall be done for them by My Father who is in heaven. For where two or three have gathered together in My name, there I am in their midst" (Matthew 18:18-20). These words encourage church leaders to humbly acknowledge their complete dependence on Christ in protecting God's children by assuring them that those who so lead will be used as God's instruments to accomplish His purposes.[2]

Humility Involves Paying the Debt of Forgiveness

During the course of Jesus' teaching, Peter returned and slipped in with the other disciples to listen to Him. Suddenly, he seemed to have made an important connection. Those who protect God's people from stumbling obviously would need to forgive them on many occasions. But what about those stubborn sheep who sinned repeatedly? Just how magnanimous should leaders be? Jewish tradition obligated a person to forgive a sinner up to three times for the same offense,[3] but Jesus seemed to be advocating even greater forgiveness. Peter, not being one to ponder unanswered questions for long, piped up and asked, "Lord, how often shall my brother sin against me and I forgive him? Up to seven times?" (v. 21).

I believe Peter's intentions were good. After all, he was more than doubling the traditional requirement and no doubt thought he was being very gracious indeed. Therefore, he must have been shocked by his Master's response: "I do not say to you, up to seven times, but up to seventy times seven" (v. 22). Then He launched into a parable illustrating the way in which those who enter the kingdom of heaven through the door of humility incur a *debt of forgiveness* which God expects them to pay.

He told of a king who, while settling accounts with his slaves, forgave one of them a huge unpayable debt. This slave then went out and encountered a fellow slave who owed him a much smaller payable debt. Instead of "passing on" the mercy he had received, the first slave refused to forgive his fellow slave and had him thrown into prison. Obviously, the first slave's desire for revenge was greater than his need to be repaid! When the king was informed about this behavior, he summoned the unmerciful slave for another accounting. Since he was unwilling to extend the same mercy he had received, he would be turned over to the torturers "until he should repay all that was owed him" (v. 34).

Jesus concluded by telling his disciples, "So shall My heavenly Father also do to you, if each of you does not forgive his brother from your heart" (v. 35). Jesus' point was that those who are forgiven by God when they are adopted into His family acquire an obligation to forgive as they have been forgiven (Ephesians 4:32). This payable debt of forgiveness replaces the unpayable debt of sin that was canceled. Failure to pay this new debt results in some pretty stiff consequences — things like stress, hardship, and guilt — that are disciplinary in nature and intended to motivate the delinquent believer to shoulder his legitimate obligations.

God's children in general and their leaders in particular are called to reflect the glory of their redemption in Christ, at the heart of which lies forgiveness of sin. Christians who refuse to forgive do not demonstrate their new nature in Christ and must be corrected. Jesus, in teaching His disciples this parable, was not only admonishing them to be forgiving.

He was also telling them to take care of God's kids by teaching and modeling forgiveness before them.

Notes:

1. Walter A. Elwell, ed., *Evangelical Dictionary of Theology* (Grand Rapids, Mich.: Baker Book House, 1984), 537.

2. These verses are often referenced in connection with prayer; however, their immediate context is a discussion of the church discipline process. Although prayer is, of course, an integral part of this process, Matthew 18:18-20 promises humble church leaders the wisdom they need to deal righteously with sinning believers. These verses are not a "blank check" guaranteed by corporate prayer meetings.

3. John MacArthur, Jr., *The MacArthur New Testament Commentary: Matthew 16-23* (Chicago, Ill.: Moody Press, 1988), 145.

Review Questions

1. Read Matthew 17:22-23 and Mark 9:30-32. Then explain how the response of Jesus' disciples to the "bad news" of the Cross temporarily deafened them to the good news of the Gospel.

2. What is the essence of humility? With that essence in mind, explain John Calvin's belief that *humility alone exalts God as sovereign.* Then explain how humility stimulates appreciation for the magnitude of God's grace.

3. Read Matthew 17:24-27 and 1 Peter 2:11-17. How did the miracle Jesus performed in the Matthew passage help Peter learn a critical lesson about humility? What does the 1 Peter passage tell you about how well he learned that lesson?

4. Describe some of the qualities of childlike humility that make it a prerequisite for entering the kingdom of heaven. Then explain Jesus' statement: "Whoever then humbles himself as this little child, he is the greatest in the kingdom of heaven" (Matthew 18:4).

5. Why must spiritual leaders be intensely concerned about the welfare of God's precious children? Describe some ways spiritual leaders should express their concern for those they lead. Explain the essential role of humility in spiritual leadership. Is intense concern for the welfare of God's precious children required only of church leaders? Why or why not? (NOTE: Consider who can be reasonably included in the term "spiritual leaders.")

6. Discuss the importance of paying the debt of forgiveness that all Christians incur when they come into God's Kingdom. According to Jesus, is this debt ever marked "paid in full"?

Applying the Word

1. This week review the verses you have memorized from previous lessons. Then begin memorizing one or more of the following:

   Psalm 8:1-9
   Micah 6:8
   1 Peter 2:11-12

2. How do you usually respond to extremely bad news? Does your typical response reflect humble submission to God's sovereign control over your life? Give several specific examples to support your answer. Then list several reasons why it is important for you to demonstrate humility in the ways in which you respond to the circumstances of life. What changes do you need to make that will help you demonstrate greater humility in your attitudes and behavior? When and where will you begin implementing these changes? Who loves you enough to encourage you and hold you accountable for making these changes? When will you share your plan with this person?

3. How much humility does God see in you? Consider this question carefully by asking yourself:

   What legitimate rights have I willingly foregone to avoid giving unnecessary offense?
   How often do I complain about governmental, business, or familial authority?
   Do I submit easily to those who occupy God-given positions of authority over me? (This would include government officials, ordained church leaders, employ-

ers, husbands, and parents who are *not* asking you to violate specific scriptural commands.)

Do I freely acknowledge my complete dependence upon God?

Do I live consistently with my acknowledgment of complete dependence upon God?

Do I exhibit deep concern for the welfare of all of God's children? (Since all Christians are "spiritual leaders" in some situations, this applies to all Christians.)

Do I consider how my actions or attitudes may cause other believers to stumble?

Am I more grieved by my own sins than I am by the sins of others?

Am I willing to assist my church leaders in going after stray sheep?

Do I cooperate with those who come after me when I stray?

Am I willing to go to a sinning brother or sister and gently plead with them to repent?

Do I repent readily when others confront me with my sin?

Do I express my gratitude to those who biblically confront me with my sin?

Do I readily forgive others as I have been forgiven by God?

In answering these questions, give specific examples. Then note those areas where you are most lacking in humility. Ask God to help you select one or two areas in which to begin working to develop deeper humility. Enlist the support of a relative, mentor, or close friend to help you make needed changes.

Digging Deeper

1. Most commentators agree that the parable Jesus taught in Matthew 18:23-35 addresses the responsibility of Christians to forgive as they have been forgiven. Some go on to say that the parable also teaches that Christians who do not carry out this responsibility stand in danger of losing their salvation. Others say that the parable teaches that believers who do not carry out this responsibility will be firmly disciplined by God but stand in no danger of losing their salvation. Study this passage in context (the immediate context and the whole context of Scripture), consult reputable commentaries, and discuss this parable with one or more of your church leaders. Then explain which interpretation best represents what Scripture (the whole counsel of God) teaches.

2. Is there a significant difference between being *childlike* and being *childish* in response to spiritual truth? If so, explain.

*"He is no fool who gives what he cannot keep
to gain what he cannot lose."*

❧

Jim Elliot

Chapter 8

The Wise Investment of Sacrifice

(Bible reading: Genesis 11:27-12:5, 22:1-19;
Matthew 19:16-20:16; Mark 10:17-31; Luke 18:18-30; 19:1-10;
1 Timothy 6:17-19; Hebrews 11:8-10, 17-19)

As Jesus and His disciples were traveling through Perea on their way to Jerusalem, a young man suddenly ran up and knelt before Jesus. "Good Teacher," he said. "What shall I do to inherit eternal life?"

Has anyone ever asked you a question like that? Right off the bat? Out of the blue? Without one single word of "pre-evangelism" preparation? Probably not. Rarely do Christians encounter such a hot prospect. Most of the Christians I know spend far more time planting seeds than they do reaping a harvest. If you're in that category, stop and think for a moment about how you would have responded to Jesus' prospect.

Would you have stuffed your four spiritual laws or your two EE questions back into your notebook and jumped right to "closure"? Would you have whipped out your well-worn copy of The Sinner's Prayer and told him to "just repeat after me and you've got it!"? Would you have gripped him fervently by the hand and assured him that all he had to do was "believe in Jesus Christ"? If so, you might want to turn in your WWJD bracelet. Amazingly, Jesus was not the least bit inclined to close this deal quickly. In fact, He appears to have deliberately discouraged the young man's hot pursuit of eternal life.

Jesus' response to what most of us would consider the "perfect question" is downright astounding: "Why do you call Me good?" He asked. "No one is good except God alone. You know the commandments, 'Do not murder, do not commit adultery, do not steal, do not bear false witness, do not defraud, honor your father and mother'" (Mark 10:18-19). At first glance it may seem that our Lord was denying both His own deity and God's gospel of grace, but a bit deeper thought reveals that He wasn't. Actually, He was asking this man, "Do you recognize Me as God in the flesh? And do you acknowledge that I have come to fulfill all of God's righteous requirements on your behalf because you can't do that yourself?"

We'd be safe to say that Jesus' astounding response was a fully appropriate "set-up" — skillfully used to expose the heart attitude behind the young man's seemingly excellent question. Obviously, the young man was sincere. Luke tells us he was a "ruler," probably a synagogue official, and therefore a man of dignity and stature in the community. And yet, he ran up to Jesus, knelt before Him, and admitted (publicly) his lack of spiritual fullness. He also had come to the right source with the right question. He had probably heard of Jesus' teachings and knew that this "good teacher" had the words of eternal life. Who better to ask how he might inherit it?

Jesus, however, refused to apply Gospel salve to felt needs when heart surgery was indicated. The young man's self-righteous assertion that he had kept all the commandments from his youth up revealed his utter insensitivity to his own sinfulness. Clearly, he had yet to see his own righteousness exposed as filthy rags in the pure light of God's holiness. He had not measured himself against God's perfect standard and come away wanting. To paraphrase John MacArthur's words of commentary, he had not yet despaired of his own efforts, nor had he seen himself as a living violation of God's holiness. He had not come to confess and throw himself on God's mercy, acknowledging that he had nothing good to offer. Nor had he come realizing that anything good he would ever receive or accomplish could come only through God's sovereign, gracious provision in Jesus Christ.[1]

Jesus essentially doused this hot prospect with freezing cold water when He told him pointblank: "One thing you lack; go and sell all you possess, and give to the poor, and you shall have treasure in heaven; and come, follow Me" (v. 21). Was Jesus espousing a gospel of works? Would the young man's obedience to this command assure him of salvation? No to both questions. Rather, Jesus' command deftly exposed the young man's heart of stone. As he walked away grieving because he owned so much property, it was clear that his goods, not the Lord, were his chosen master. His desire for God's fullest blessing was no doubt sincere, but the high price of submission to absolute sovereignty was more than he wanted to pay.

Why Throw Cold Water on a Hot Prospect?

Jesus' evangelistic technique wouldn't pass muster in many churches these days. Christians, in general, are more likely to grease the skids into the kingdom of heaven than to intentionally toss roadblocks before a hot prospect. For the most part, our *motives* aren't bad. We want to see people saved. We want to see churches grow. We want to see lives change for the better. Above all, we want to see God honored and glorified. Given those good desires, building heart-scrutiny into evangelism seems a bit counterproductive. After all, if we want to see all those good things happen, shouldn't we make it as easy as possible for hot prospects to get into the Kingdom?

Hard as my answer may be to hear, I would say *No, we shouldn't — because Jesus didn't.*

We can be sure that His methods were perfect because He always did the will of the Father (John 4:34, 8:29). God had established His Kingdom's entrance requirements before time began, and Jesus refused to relax them when He walked the earth. Since Father and Son were One in essence, they worked harmoniously to accomplish salvation. Jesus presented the Gospel message to folks for what it actually was — the only remedy for bondage to sin, not as what many would like it to be — the solution to all their felt needs and desires.

The young man who knelt before Jesus somewhere in Perea was seeking salvation for all the wrong reasons.

He wasn't concerned (or even aware) that his sinful state made him offensive to God. He didn't see his real need for the cleansing forgiveness of full atonement. He hadn't yet reached the point of hating his sin so intensely that he would gladly give all that he owned to be free of its grip. Rather, he was seeking to add eternal life to all the good stuff he already had. Although He knew that good stuff hadn't been able to fill a troublesome hole in his heart, he was unwilling to part with all that good stuff in order to fill it.

Jesus' confrontational evangelism had clearly revealed that this seemingly hot prospect was still a long way from "white unto harvest." I imagine deep sadness in our Lord's eyes and voice when he turned to His disciples and said, "How hard it is for those who are wealthy to enter the kingdom of God!" (Mark 10:23). The Twelve were amazed. Apparently, like so many of us, they had considered great wealth to be a decided advantage in all areas of life. They were probably wondering how poor men like themselves would be able to enter the Kingdom if the rich found it difficult.

Jesus picked up on their musings and added these words, "Children, how hard it is to enter the kingdom of God! It is easier for a camel to go through the eye of a needle than for a rich man to enter the kingdom of God." Now the disciples were truly disturbed. "Then who can be saved?" they asked in astonishment (vv. 24-26).

Jesus' reply summed up the point of his encounter with the young man. "With men it is impossible, but not with God; for all things are possible with God" (v. 27). The fact is that no one can be saved by personal effort. Salvation is wholly an act of God. It is received by those who respond in God-given faith (Ephesians 2:8-9; 2 Peter 1:1) to the convicting power of God's Holy Spirit (John 16:8). And it demands full dependence on God's perfect provision for cleansing forgiveness from the pollution of sin.

Those who are rich find humble submission to God's absolute sovereignty especially difficult because they are used to relying on their wealth and possessions. They have great confidence in their own abilities and are unaccustomed to relying on others. They are likely to think that salvation's price tag is truly exorbitant. However, God's power is mighty to save even the rich. Men like Abraham and Zaccheus have been blessed with a godly perspective of riches and would heartily agree with Charles Spurgeon who said, "Oh that we may never hesitate to be glad losers for Jesus! They who lose all for Christ will find all in Christ and receive all with Christ."[2]

Great wealth is only one of the idols that keep men and women from giving all to possess the pearl of great price. Our evangelism techniques should uncover those idols and seek to destroy them, rather than misleading idolaters into thinking that they can keep all their idols and have Jesus too.

What About Us?

For once, Peter seems to have quickly gotten the point of what Jesus was teaching. He and the other disciples *had* willingly paid the price that the rich young man had considered too high. Thus, they could lay claim to promised treasure in heaven. It was only natural for Peter to wonder what that treasure was like. "Behold," he asked Jesus, "We have left everything and followed You; what then will there be for us?" (Matthew 19:27).

Some commentators attribute the most mercenary of motives to Peter's question, but I must respectfully beg to differ with them. Since I have no way of discerning the state of the Fisherman's heart at that moment, I defer to the One who knew all about him. Jesus was not at all hesitant to rebuke His disciple when his sinful heart needed it, but in this case, the Lord answered his question without a hint of correction.

"Truly, I say to you," Jesus told Peter, "that you who have followed Me, in the regeneration when the Son of Man will sit on His glorious throne, you also shall sit upon twelve thrones, judging the twelve tribes of Israel. And everyone who has left houses or brothers or sisters or father or mother or children or farms for My name's sake, shall receive many times as much, and shall inherit eternal life. But many who are first will be last; and the last, first" (vv. 28-30). Apparently Jesus saw nothing wrong with Peter's desire to know about his reward. Instead of reproving him for his curiosity, the Lord greatly encouraged him (and the others) with a detailed description of what they could expect in return for their faithfulness.

The devotion exhibited by faithful disciples of Christ would be well rewarded — so well rewarded, in fact, that their fallen perspective of fairness would be stretched to the breaking point. *Everyone* Jesus called to be His disciple would receive, as the *minimum* reward, eternal life. Then rewards for service would be piled up on that one. Anyone who made sacrifices for Christ in this life would receive, in addition to eternal life, "a hundred times as much" in return both in this age and in the age to come (Mark 10:30).

A. B. Bruce, in his book *The Training of the Twelve*, waxes quite eloquent when he suggests that in the light of this promise, Jesus' requirement of faithfulness is not at all onerous. He says, "Life sacrificed on these terms is but a river emptying itself into the ocean."[3] Sinclair Ferguson, in his commentary on Mark, waxes a little less eloquent but equally memorable when he says that we should consider our sacrifices for Christ, not in terms of subtraction, but of multiplication![4]

The disciples themselves, because of their special service, would receive a special reward, that of sitting on twelve thrones to judge the twelve tribes of Israel. Peter and the other disciples may have taken this promise to mean that each of them would rule over a tribe in a restored kingdom of Israel (see Acts 1:6); however, hindsight reveals that their Lord had something different in mind. Although reputable commentators fail to agree on the precise meaning of this particular promise, most explain it in terms of the unique apostolic authority these men would wield in Christ's Church down through the centuries and into eternity.

Is it wrong to serve Jesus while anticipating reward? Apparently not. Jesus knew that discipleship would entail painful self-sacrifice and that those who followed Him faithfully would need great encouragement to help them endure. He understood that the key to joyful pursuit of God's kingdom lay in looking past all the sacrifice to what lies beyond it. The writer of Hebrews tells us that Jesus Himself "endured the cross" by fixing His mind on the "joy set before Him" (12:2). His glorious example of sacrifice motivated by joyous anticipation of what lay ahead should be ever before us as our rivers of life continue to flow over harsh, rocky shoals into His deep, tranquil ocean.

The First, the Last, and the Paycheck

Jesus then used a parable to teach His disciples that their anticipated rewards, although fully theirs, were, nevertheless, theirs only by grace. He told of a wealthy landowner who went into the marketplace four times during the day to hire idle men to work in his vineyard. The first man he hired agreed to work the whole day for a denarius, while those later hired agreed to work for "whatever is right." At the end of the day, the landowner instructed his foreman to distribute the wages, paying the last hired first and the first hired last.

When the first hired saw that the last hired were each receiving a denarius, they happily assumed that they would get more. But when they also received a single denarius for working all day, they became angry and began to grumble at the landowner accusing him of unfairness. He responded by reminding them of their agreement and by affirming his right to do what he wished with his own possessions. They were jealous, he pointed out rightly, not because he was unfair, but because he had generously elevated those last-hired to the first-hired's level.

I've seen many Christians trip over this parable by isolating it from its context and thus missing its point. Jesus used it to illustrate a great spiritual truth about eternal life, not sound economic theory about running a business. He is not saying that all factory or farm workers should receive the same pay without regard for the amount of work that they do. Rather, He is saying that eternal life is God's gracious gift, completely unearned and undeserved; and that therefore, no Christian's service warrants more eternal life than another.

The parable was part of Jesus' answer to Peter's question about treasure in heaven, and highlights the fact that *everything* about the kingdom of heaven is thoroughly gracious. The vineyard in the parable represents the kingdom itself, the landowner is God, the foreman is Christ, the laborers are believers, the denarius is eternal life, the workday is the believer's lifetime, and the end of the workday represents eternity. The call to work in the vineyard, the length of time given to work, the ability to work, and the reward for the work, are all received by God's grace rather than merit.

Most of us realize that we can't merit or earn the reward of eternal life, but we often forget that neither can we merit or earn the call to work, nor a long lifetime in which to work, nor the God-given ability to do God's work. Faithful discipleship is just as gracious as is its reward. Charles Spurgeon reminds us that "it is a great privilege to be serving the Lord throughout a long life and those who have enjoyed this high favor are deeply indebted to the grace of God."[5] Those who work longest and hardest to receive their denarius surely should count the ongoing receipt of abounding, abundant, sufficient grace for every good deed (2 Corinthians 9:8) a *great blessing* instead of a bitter inequity.

Jesus seems to be reminding the Twelve that they are among the first hired to work in the vineyard of God. They would engage in hard toil and bear the heat of the day, whereas others would work shorter (and perhaps easier) hours for exactly the same "eternal-life paycheck." Although they would enjoy a "bonus" for their unique faithfulness, their call to serve God as well as their ability to serve Him well was also due to God's grace alone. By their own efforts, they would be unable to merit any reward at all. As they worked hard in God's vineyard, they would be sorely tempted by both envy and pride, and yielding to either would hamper their service. Jesus' teaching this day would help them remember that their best defense against these vile adversaries would be cultivating a mindset of deep love and gratitude for the unparalleled riches of freely bestowed grace.

Notes:

1. John MacArthur, Jr., *The MacArthur New Testament Commentary: Matthew 16-23* (Chicago, Ill.: Moody Press, 1988), 192.

2. Charles Haddon Spurgeon, *The Gospel of Matthew*, Larry Richards, gen. ed. (Grand Rapids, Mich.: Fleming H. Revell, 1987), 272.

3. A. B. Bruce, *The Training of the Twelve* (Grand Rapids, Mich.: Kregel Publications, 1971, 1988), 268.

4. Sinclair B. Ferguson, *Let's Study Mark* (Carlisle, Penn.: The Banner of Truth Trust, 1999), 169.

5. Spurgeon, 277.

Review Questions

1. Describe Jesus' surprising response to the "hot prospect" He encountered in Perea. According to the gospel accounts of this incident, what motivated Jesus to respond to this young man as He did?

2. Was Jesus advocating a gospel of works when He told the young man to sell all he possessed and then to come and follow Him? Explain.

3. Discuss the wisdom of occasionally (or perhaps routinely) "throwing cold water on a hot prospect." Include Jesus' illustration about camels in your discussion.

4. Read Genesis 11:27-12:5, 22:1-19, Luke 19:1-10, and Hebrews 11:8-10, 17-19. Compare the responses of Abraham and Zaccheus (who were wealthy men) to God with the response of the rich young man described in this lesson to Christ. To what do you attribute the differences in their responses? Support your answer with Scripture.

5. Is it wrong to serve Jesus while anticipating rewards? Support your answer with Scripture.

6. How did the parable of the workers in the vineyard help to prepare the disciples for the work God had chosen them to do?

Applying the Word

1. Devote this week to reviewing the verses you have memorized in previous lessons.

2. Examine your own evangelistic techniques in light of this lesson. Are you more inclined to grease the skids into the kingdom of heaven than you are to throw roadblocks before hot prospects? Explain. Prayerfully examine the motives behind your particular inclination. Are those motives God-honoring? Self-protective? Self-exalting? Confess any motivational sin of which you have been convicted and receive God's cleansing forgiveness. Then consider how your evangelistic techniques should be adjusted or revised to include a call to heart scrutiny by "hot prospects." Then write out an approach to evangelism that includes a call to heart scrutiny in accord with the biblical gospel. If you need help with this exercise, consult your pastor, one of your church leaders, a close friend, or a mentor who is gifted in evangelism.

3. Describe your view of rewards in God's service. Does your view coincide with Jesus' answer to Peter's question? If so, thank God for the riches of His grace. If not, prayerfully consider various ways in which your view should change in order to conform more closely to what Jesus taught Peter and the other disciples.

Digging Deeper

1. Write an essay entitled, "How to Not Be a Fool," in which you relate Jim Elliot's quote, which opens this chapter, to the biblical account of the rich young ruler.

"[Love is] the mark that Jesus gives to label a Christian
not just in one era or in one locality
but at all times and all places until Jesus returns."

Frances Schaeffer

Chapter 9

Learning To Love

---

*(Bible reading: Leviticus 19:18; Deuteronomy 6:5;
Psalm 35:11-16; Matthew 26:14-25; Mark 14:10-21;
Luke 22:1-13; John 13:1-35; 1 Corinthians 13:4-8a;
Philippians 2:5-11; 1 John 4:7-21)*

I wonder if Peter was fighting an ominous sense of foreboding as he surveyed the large, upper guest room where he and the others would celebrate Passover with Jesus. I wonder if he surreptitiously studied John's face and demeanor to see if he felt it too. Although the two of them shared privileged closeness with Jesus, John's heart-ties with the Master were especially tender. If something was up, John probably knew it.

Jesus had sent them into the city that day to make preparations for Passover. "When you have entered the city," He said, "a man will meet you carrying a pitcher of water; follow him into the house he enters. And you shall say to the owner of the house, 'The Teacher says to you, "Where is the guest room in which I may eat the Passover with My disciples?"' And he will show you a large, furnished, upper room; prepare it there" (Luke 22:10-12).

Peter may well have discussed his uneasiness with his fellow disciple as they made preparations for the Passover meal. Although the Gospels provide us no clue as to their conversation, surely their minds kept returning to Jesus' affirmations that He would die in this city. I wonder if these two close disciples of Jesus unconsciously tried to postpone the inevitable by working slowly that day and perhaps even dragging their feet as they returned to tell Jesus that their assigned task was completed.

Later that evening as the men filed into the room and took their places around the large, laden table, Peter probably smiled to see John in his usual spot — on Jesus' right, close to His heart. He may have nodded to Judas Iscariot, their treasurer, who, on this evening, occupied the traditional place of honor on Jesus' left. Then he probably frowned as he noted the conspicuous absence of the house-slave who should have been ready upon their arrival to wash the dirt from their feet before they started to eat.

The other disciples had no doubt noticed the slave's absence also. Although Scripture is silent about their specific behavior, I imagine their conversations growing self-consciously animated as time went by and no slave appeared. I picture a room full of proud men encumbered by grimy feet and desperately trying to look far too important to notice the untended basin and towel in the corner. I see each man occasionally cut his eyes toward the door or the basin and then quickly return to his VIP interactions.

I also see Jesus watching them closely. Would any one of them act on what He had taught them about love and humility? *No, none of them would.* Apparently, they had not made the connection between knowledge and actions. William Hendriksen says, "The fact that greatness is measured with the yardstick of service had not registered with them."[1] After all Jesus had taught them about servant leadership, none of His leaders-in-training were willing to humble themselves in the presence of others. Rather than stoop to a servant's position, they preferred to recline at the table in the unsavory company of dirt-covered feet.

Jesus allowed the meal to begin, and then quietly rose from His place. As He walked toward the basin and towel, I'm sure all conversation immediately ceased. By the time Jesus had disrobed, girded Himself with the towel, and knelt to unlatch the first pair of sandals, the silence must have been thoroughly deafening. In my mind's eye, I see twenty-four horrified eyes locked on the kneeling figure of Jesus. I see twelve stunned disciples, too shocked to eat, move, or speak, asking themselves, "What in the world is He doing?" I see John's eyes filling with tears, Judas's jaw setting like flint, and Peter's face slowly turning an angry beet-red.

What in the world *was* Jesus doing? Something far more important than cleaning their feet. His stunning behavior was carefully calculated to shatter their prideful pretensions and teach them a practical lesson well-seasoned with theological truth. First, He would command their undivided attention by *demonstrating* the inherent connection between love and humility. And then He would elaborate on that essential connection by revealing some truths about the love with which God had loved them and with which they ought to love one another. He would teach them by word and deed that such love isn't dignified nor is it treacherous, but it is highly distinctive.

Love Isn't Dignified

The Apostle John, writing many years later with Spirit-inspired perspective and insight, hangs an enlightening backdrop behind the events of that evening. He tells us that, as Jesus observed the proud posturing of His slow-learning disciples, He was sure of three things. First, He knew that His hour had come. Having loved "His own in the world...to the end," it was now time for Him to depart and return to the Father. Second, He knew that His betrayer had cast his lot with the devil. Although Jesus would pursue Judas in love to the very last moment and thus glorify God, He knew that the traitor would refuse to relent. And third, Jesus knew that all things had been given into His hands, that He had come from God, and that He was going back to God. He had absolutely no doubts about who He was nor about what He was doing.

When Jesus got up from the table to wash twenty-four dirty, arrogant feet, it wasn't because He had momentarily forgotten that He was God in the flesh. He did it because time was short, and because "His own in the world" needed to learn that love isn't dignified. He did it to show them that love couldn't care less about how it looks to others, and couldn't care more about meeting the needs of those others. To borrow a phrase from William Temple, He did it to show them that "When a man stands on his dignity, he usually succeeds in squashing it flat."[2] Jesus wanted His proud disciples to see clearly that their guarded dignity looked pretty wretched to the loving God who had saved them by humbling His Son.

Jesus had not stood on the dignity of His eternal existence in the form of God, but stooped instead to take on the form of a bond-servant in the likeness of men. He then secured the salvation of God's chosen children through His humble obedience to the point of death on a cross. His willing refusal to guard His own dignity earned Him high exaltation and receipt of the name which is above every name (Philippians 2:6-11). Therefore, as Jesus washed dirty arrogant feet, He was not only teaching His men to humbly love one another, He was also giving them an unforgettably graphic depiction of His mission among them. He had not come to be served, but to serve, and those who would call Him Savior and Lord must have the same mindset.

The men in the room with Jesus that night watched in pained silence as He taught them this lesson...all of them except Peter, that is. As Jesus approached Peter's place at the table, the outspoken disciple protested indignantly. Peter was, after all, the foundation stone of the Church, and therefore believed he should guard Jesus' dignity even more closely than he did his own. Jesus seemed to have respected Peter's concern when He calmly assured him, "What I do you do not realize now, but you shall understand hereafter" (John 13:7). Peter, however, preferred his own judgment to that of his Lord. "Never shall You wash my feet!" he affirmed to the God-Man kneeling humbly before him.

This wasn't the first time that Peter had overstepped his authority by correcting His Lord; and once again, I believe that he spoke without weighing the full implications of what he was saying. He seemed unaware of the fact that the stand he was taking effectively excised the essence of Jesus' ministry.

Humility (to the point of humiliation) was required to provide atonement for sin. Jesus had already humbled Himself in the Incarnation and would humble Himself even more by dying for His elect. Washing the feet of His disciples was simply a picture of His work among them. By refusing the picture, Peter had also thoughtlessly rebuffed the reality. Peter's lack of submission to His Master's humility amounted to open rebellion against His authority.

Jesus' humiliation in no way negated His Lordship. Redeeming a people *for His own possession* required them to submit to His sovereign rule. Those who would be His possession don't have the option of spurning His will simply because they don't understand it or fail to agree with it. Peter couldn't have Jesus as Savior and refuse Him as Lord. Jesus the Savior is, *by definition*, Christ the Lord (Luke 2:11); thus, His elect can relate to Him in no other way.

Jesus knew Peter's words had been thoughtlessly spoken. And He loved him enough to shock him back to his senses. "If I do not wash you, you have no part with Me," He bluntly told the foundation stone of His church. Peter seemed to have gotten the message immediately. "Lord, not my feet only, but also my hands and my head" (John 13:8-9). I can almost hear Jesus chuckle as He reassured this solid saint who was so given to extremes of devotion: "He who has bathed needs only to wash his feet, but is completely clean; and you are clean, but not all of you" (v. 10).

Jesus was reminding Peter that just as he had bathed his whole body before attending the dinner and only needed some dirt removed from his feet, he had also received the bath of salvation and only needed forgiveness for ongoing sins. Since Christ would pay the Law's penalty for all of his sins, Peter was privileged to call God his Father instead of his Judge (Romans 5:6-11). And since Jesus would pay, once and for all, the full debt of his sin, Peter's place in God's family was absolutely secure (Romans 8:31-39; 2 Timothy 1:12). Ongoing forgiveness would be needed, however, to maintain a harmonious family relationship (1 John 1:9).

After completing His task and settling back into His place at the table, Jesus admonished them all to follow His example of selfless, loving service. If they would obey, He assured them, they would be greatly blessed (John 13:17). They would know the unequaled joy of fruitful hard work accomplished for the most majestic of purposes. They would escape the soul-wrenching guilt of neglecting to do what they knew to be right. And they would delight in the whole-hearted approval of their beloved Lord and Savior.

Tragically however, not all of them would be greatly blessed, because one of them was a traitor. Jesus told them, "I know the ones I have chosen; but it is that the Scripture may be fulfilled, 'He who eats my bread has lifted up his heel against Me.' From now on I am telling you before it comes to pass, so that when it does occur, you may believe that I am He." Jesus had known from the very beginning the name of the one who would fulfill scriptural prophecy by betraying Him to His enemies. The man known by that name had been chosen, in fact, for that very purpose (John 6:70-71). Jesus now wanted His disciples to know that He knew about the traitor among them so that when he was unmasked, their faith wouldn't waiver.

Love Isn't Treacherous

Discussing the traitor was troubling for Jesus. Scripture gives us no reason to think that Jesus loved Judas Iscariot any less than He loved the other disciples. And yet He knew that this man would respond to His love with unspeakable treachery — and thereby unwittingly play a key role in God's eternal plan of salvation. Judas, however, would not be rewarded for his part in God's plan because his actions were motivated by greed, power, and malice. He would not play his role with a heart humbly submitted to God's sovereign will, but rather with a mind firmly set on his own sinful agenda.

Since God's sovereign power extends to all creatures, He frequently uses the willful rebellion of unsaved men and women to accomplish His purposes, and then righteously judges them guilty of damnable sin. Jesus grieved over Judas because, although He loved him, He knew the betrayer would reap what he had sown. "It would have been good for that man," He told His disciples, "if he had not been born" (Matthew 26:24).

Jesus' love for His betrayer led Him to treat Judas the same way that He did the other disciples during three years of ministry. The shocked response of the men to His announcement of a traitor among them testifies to that fact. Apparently, Jesus' interaction with Judas had given them no reason to single him out as the betrayer. To their credit, the men seemed to suspect their own loyalty more than they did any one else's. Perhaps Jesus' vivid lessons that evening had, after all, had an impact upon them.

Peter, too disturbed to waste time speculating about who the traitor might be, gestured to John — indicating that he should ask Jesus pointblank for the name of the blackguard. Peter no doubt believed that if Jesus would divulge that information to anyone, He would divulge it to John. And he was right. The two men were close enough, in both location and heart, for Jesus to quietly speak into the ear of the disciple He loved, "That is the one for whom I shall dip the morsel and give it to him" (John 13:26).

My guess is that John was unable to communicate Jesus' words to the curious fisherman before the dipped morsel was handed to Judas. Given Peter's self-assertive track record, if he had known that Judas was "it," he would no doubt have been two steps behind him with blood in his eye as he left the room! Since he was not, I assume that all the disciples save John thought that Jesus was merely dispatching Judas on some pressing errand when He told him, "What you do, do quickly." Apparently, they all took the giving of the dipped morsel to be nothing more than what it was traditionally — a token gesture of respect and honor. Only Jesus and John could have seen it for what it was actually — the horrific seal of Judas's doom.

Do you ever wonder how Judas could have walked for three years with Jesus without responding to His perfect love in true saving faith? If so, you may find James Montgomery Boice's keen insights as helpful as I did. He says that it takes more than a good example to bring folks to salvation.[3] People are not converted by merely watching the lifestyles of the saved and committed. They are not converted by merely hearing the Gospel. Before they can be saved, they must be regenerated. And regeneration is wholly an act of

God (Ezekiel 36:23-28; John 6:65). Without God's sovereign action, no amount of example, persuasion, or exhortation can pump life-giving faith into dead hearts of stone.

Judas was never saved because he was never regenerated. God, in His sovereign good pleasure, chose to extend righteous justice to Judas instead of merciful grace. Although Judas walked for three years in the presence of Jesus, his steps were guided by a heart of cold stone. Since his unresponsive hard heart was never softened by God, he was completely incapable of truly loving the Savior. His incomprehensible treachery bears witness to that.

But the thing I find most amazing is that Jesus loved him in spite of that fact! Most of us don't tend to love folks who are bent on destroying us...and yet Scripture gives no indication that Jesus didn't love Judas. How could that be? Obviously, the love with which Jesus loved Judas was something quite different from the love with which sinners tend to love one another. It was divine love so distinctive that when we love as He did, we will be clearly recognized as God's chosen children.

Love Is Distinctive

Was it foolish of Jesus to love Judas, knowing full well that he had been chosen as a vessel of wrath?[4] Was Jesus' love effectively wasted by being poured out on a man whom He knew would not be won by it? No, I think not. You see, Jesus always acted in ways that were pleasing to God (John 8:29) because His ultimate purpose in coming to earth was to glorify God.

Jesus' love was extended to Judas, not in a valiant but vain effort to change God's preordained plan, but wholly and solely to glorify Him.

Loving our enemies glorifies God because in order to do it, we need God's power working in and through us. When Jesus taught His disciples to love their enemies, He told them that in so doing they would distinguish themselves from worldly, self-centered Gentiles (Matthew 5:43-47). Jesus had set the standard of such God-honoring love in His dealings with Judas; and after dismissing the betrayer to pursue his vile mission, Jesus instructed the faithful eleven to imitate His example of loving others *distinctively*.

Jesus told them that He was about to be glorified, and that in His glorification, God the Father would also be glorified (John 13:31-32). His own glorification would occur on the cross when His full and final atonement reversed the sinful conduct of Adam (Romans 5:18), broke the power of death held by Satan (Hebrews 2:14), and turned the history of mankind completely around. Having accomplished His purpose in coming to earth, He would be resurrected and then ascend to the right hand of the Father where He would rule heaven and earth with all authority. God would be glorified in Jesus' sacrifice as divine justice was satisfied through merciful grace (Romans 3:26), as God's faithfulness to His covenant promise was demonstrated (Genesis 3:14), and as His own distinctive love for His children was actively manifested (Romans 5:8).[5]

But then Jesus dropped the proverbial bombshell. His imminent glorification meant that He would only be with them a little while longer. "You shall seek Me," He said, "and as I said to the Jews, I now say to you also, 'Where I am going, you cannot come'" (John 13:33). I can't help but wonder how the men sitting around the table that night took His announcement. Surely, they scarcely grasped the significance of "glorification," and recoiled from the thought of parting company with Him. I imagine that none of the men at that table were pondering the wonders of glorification, but were more likely thinking, *What in the world are we supposed to do without Jesus?*

Jesus, of course, knew that their thoughts were running wildly in that direction, and so He proceeded to tell them precisely *what they were supposed to be doing* while He was in Heaven. Since He would no longer be with them, reflecting God's love in the earthly realm, they *were supposed* to take over that task. They would remain on the earth and love one another the way that He had loved them.

"A new commandment I give to you," Jesus said, "that you love one another, even as I have loved you, that you also love one another. By this all men will know that you are My disciples, if you have love for one another" (vv. 34-35). The men may have wondered what was so new about this commandment. After all, God's law commanded them to love their neighbors as they loved themselves (Leviticus 19:18), to do good to their enemies (Exodus 23:4-5; Psalm 35:11-16), and to love God with all their heart, soul, and might (Deuteronomy 6:5).

Of course, Jesus knew that "love one another" was an old commandment, but He was infusing it with new richness of meaning. He was declaring that they now had a living example to follow — the way in which He had lived out God's love in His Incarnation. As they patterned their love for others after His love for them, they would point people to Christ as the grand demonstration of God's perfect love for His children. *What in the world were they supposed to do without Jesus?* Love as He loved and thus glorify their Father God just as Jesus had done.

Notes:

1. William Hendriksen, *New Testament Commentary: John* (Grand Rapids, Mich.: Baker Book House, 1953), 228.

2. F. F. Bruce, *The Gospel of John* (Grand Rapids, Mich.: William B. Eerdmans Publishing Company, 1983), 284.

3. James Montgomery Boice, *The Gospel of John, vol. 4: Peace in the Storm: John 13-17* (Grand Rapids, Mich.: Baker Books, 1985, 1999), 1027.

4. See Romans 9:14-24.

5. Boice, 1033-34

Review Questions

1. Describe the reactions of Jesus' disciples to the absence of a house-slave to perform the task of foot washing. Based upon what Jesus had been teaching them (see chapters 7 & 8 of this study in particular), how should they have reacted? Support your answer with Scripture.

2. Do you think Jesus' verbal teaching about love in John 13 would have been as effective if He had not first washed His disciples' feet? Explain your answer.

3. Read Mark 10:45 and Philippians 2:5-11. Then use these verses to help you explain how "the foot washing" can be seen as a graphic depiction of the Incarnation. Then describe how both the Incarnation and the foot washing teach us that love isn't dignified.

4. Explain in your own words what Jesus meant when He told Peter, "He who has bathed needs only to wash his feet, but is completely clean."

5. Discuss several implications of the fact that Jesus became "troubled in spirit" when He told the disciples there was a traitor among them.

6. How is it possible that Judas could have walked with Jesus for three years without responding in faith to His perfect love?

7. Discuss the significance of loving others distinctively.

Applying the Word

1. This week review the verses you have memorized from previous lessons. Then begin memorizing one or more of the following:
   John 13:34-35
   1 Corinthians 13:4-8a
   1 John 4:7

2. Peter may have believed that his objection to Jesus' washing his feet was an act of humility because he thought he was "protecting" Jesus' dignity. However, John Calvin saw Peter's action as prideful and commented on it with these words: "Until a man renounces his freedom to pass judgments on God's deeds, no matter how much he may try to honor God, pride will always lurk disguised as humility" (John Calvin, *The Crossway Classic Commentaries: John*, Alister McGrath, J. I. Packer, eds. [Wheaton, Ill.: Crossway Books, 1994], 321). Describe in your own words the pride you see lurking disguised as humility in Peter's objection. Then ask the Lord in prayer to reveal ways in which pride may be lurking disguised as humility in your words, attitudes, and actions. Describe one or more of the "revelations" the Lord gives you. Use a concordance, if necessary, to find passages of Scripture that will help you become truly humble in these areas. Memorize some of these verses and ask God's Holy Spirit to bring them to mind whenever you are tempted to pride in these areas.

3. Carefully read John 13:34-35 and 1 Corinthians 13:4-8a. Then reread John 13:34-35 aloud replacing the word "you" in the passage with your name. Reread 1 Corinthians 13:4-8a aloud replacing the word "love" with

your name. Which of the "personalized" phrases in these passages were actually *untrue* of you? (Think in terms of your *usual* behavior.) Do you believe that if you "lived out" 1 Corinthians 13:4-8a, you would also obey Jesus' command in John 13:34-35? Explain your answer. (Think in terms of how *living out* 1 Corinthians 13:4-8a would *distinctively* mark you as a disciple of Christ.) Select one or two of the areas in which you *are not* living out 1 Corinthians 13:4-8a, and make a specific step by step plan that will help you to do so. Then note the areas in which you *are* living out 1 Corinthians 13:4-8a. Thank God for His faithfulness in helping you do so, and recommit to remaining faithful to Him in these areas.

Digging Deeper

1. Read 2 Samuel 15-17 and Psalm 41. What similarities do you see between David's situation with Ahithophel and Jesus's situation with Judas? Based on the similarities you see, what do you think David's motivation might have been in writing Psalm 41? What do you think Jesus' motivation might have been in quoting from Psalm 41?

2. Some people believe that it is unfair or even cruel of God to use the sinfulness of people like Judas to accomplish His purposes and then condemn them for the very sinful actions He used. Research this challenging issue related to God's absolute sovereignty and write a response explaining why such actions of God are neither unfair nor cruel. Discuss your research and your conclusions with your pastor, another of your church leaders, or a mature Christian friend or mentor.

"Saints mourn more for sin than other men."

From: *The Valley of Vision:*
A Collection of Puritan Prayers and Devotions

Chapter 10

The Agony of Denial

---

*(Bible reading: Psalm 1, 130:1-6; Jeremiah 17:9-10, 14;
Zechariah 13:7; Matthew 26:30-75; Mark 14:26-72;
Luke 22:24-62; John 13:36-14:4, 18:1-27;
1 Corinthians 10:12-13; 1 Peter 5:8-11)*

"Simon, Simon, behold, Satan has demanded permission to sift you like wheat; but I have prayed for you, that your faith may not fail; and you, when once you have turned again, strengthen your brothers."

Luke tells us that Jesus spoke these words to Peter soon after announcing that one of the Twelve would betray Him. It seems that the men's animated discussion about who the traitor might be had quickly dissolved into the recurring argument over "which one of them was regarded to be the greatest" (22:24). Jesus proceeded to correct them much as He had before (see chapter 8), then turned to Peter and uttered the startling revelation quoted above.

Although it contains one of the most glorious promises in all of Scripture, Peter apparently didn't take it that way. Instead of responding humbly with something like, "Thank you, Lord, for the comforting assurance of Your sustaining power in the gravest of trials," Peter responded quite proudly by saying, "Lord, with You I am ready to go both to prison and to death!" (v. 33) I'm not sure whether Peter was defending himself against what he saw as an affront to his loyalty, or acknowledging what he had misread as a declaration of Jesus' great confidence in him. In either case, he had missed the whole point of what Jesus was saying. And Jesus wasted no time in setting him straight. "I say to you, Peter, the cock will not crow today until you have denied three times that you know Me" (v. 34).

As was so often the case, the Lord had to use a "big stick" to get Peter's attention. Jesus knew that the fisherman's love was sincere and that his intentions were good. But He also knew that the bold courage Peter so proudly displayed sprang from his great confidence *in himself* instead of unshakable faith in the Lord. Peter was immature, and needed to grow up in a hurry. Within twenty-four hours, Jesus would be crucified, dead, and buried. And Peter would be thrust into a leadership role that would crush any man who attempted to play it without divine aid.

Jesus knew that His enemy, Satan, had insidiously targeted the foundation stone of His Church for destruction. He knew that Satan would launch his most vicious attack against Peter's most evident vulnerability — his overarching self-confidence. However, Jesus also knew that what Satan intended for evil, God would use for good.

Like all committed disciples, Peter contained a lot of good wheat along with much useless chaff. Satan desired to sift Peter through a grave trial in order to dispose of the wheat and harvest the chaff. However, his evil desire would be thwarted — because Jesus had prayed for the foundation stone of His church. R. Kent Hughes, borrowing from Alexander Maclaren, expressed it like this: "But Christ prayed for Peter, and through Peter's failure the chaff blew away and the wheat remained. Peter's vanity was sifted out, his misplaced self-confidence was sifted away, his presumption was sifted, his impulsive mouth was winnowed — and he became a great strength to his brothers and sisters in the early church."[1]

Peter would fall, and he would fall hard. But his fall was essential, both for his own welfare and the welfare of Christ's church. Without it, he would not have learned humble dependence on Jesus, and we would not have his example to follow. Peter learned the hard way that discipleship is impossible for those who trust in themselves, just as we will if we choose to ignore what happened to him.

The Gospel accounts of Peter's denial of Christ bear sobering testimony to the perils inherent in trusting weak flesh, but also encourage us with their witness to the power of God's inexhaustible grace. They warn us that even the most committed of saints can commit the most heinous of sins. And they assure us that no sin committed by a true child of God will exhaust the grace of the Father toward those He has chosen.

John's gospel is especially clear on this point. There Jesus' unsettling announcement of Peter's upcoming denial is followed immediately by these timeless words of assurance and hope: "Let not your heart be troubled; believe in God, believe also in Me. In My Father's house are many dwelling places; if it were not so, I would have told you; for I go to prepare a place for you. And if I go and prepare a place for you, I will come again, and receive you to Myself; that where I am, there you may be also" (14:1-3). We know that Jesus directed these words to the whole group because the "you's" are plural; however, I can't help but think that He spoke with a dual intention. Clearly, He was assuring them all that their separation from Him would not be permanent, but He also seems to be comforting Peter specifically with the implied promise of full forgiveness and restoration.

Peter's great fall didn't occur all at once. As is usually the case with great falls, the foundation stone of Christ's church "fell apart" one misstep at a time. Peter first tripped over his self-confident boldness, then stumbled into self-indulgent prayerlessness, and finally crashed to the ground in a flurry of self-deluding foolhardiness. As we trace his faltering steps in this lesson, let's allow his example to both convict and encourage us in our walk with the Lord.

The Trip: Self-confident Boldness

Peter appears to have been so thoroughly stunned by Jesus' prophetic warning of his impending denial that he heard little or nothing of what Jesus said afterward. Mark tells us that "Peter *kept saying insistently*, 'Even if I have to die with You, I will not deny You!'" (14:31). Apparently, he simply refused to accept Jesus' sovereign insight and foresight.

Even when Jesus told the whole group, "You will all fall away because of Me this night, because it is written, 'I will strike down the shepherd, and the sheep of the flock will be scattered'" (Matthew 26:31), Peter pursued his protest. "Even though all may fall away because of You, I will never fall away" (v. 32). Then the other disciples, perhaps more in self-defense than in confidence, began proclaiming their loyalty to Jesus as well.

I'm sure that the fisherman was completely sincere in his proclamation of faithfulness to Jesus that night. Unfortunately, sincerity is no accurate measure of spiritual strength. Peter's sincerity blinded him to the hazard of trusting in weak human flesh, and he tripped over the obstacle of self-confident boldness. He was so sure of *himself* that he disdained the importance of relying on Jesus.

So sure of himself was he, in fact, that he (once again) presumptuously contradicted God in the flesh. *Jesus, You're wrong,* he said in effect. *I don't care what You think You know about me; I will never deny You.* Then he boldly declared himself equal to any difficult trial. *Don't worry about me, Lord,* he boasted, *I'm ready for prison and I don't mind dying. No matter what's coming, You can count on me to handle it perfectly.* And finally, he arrogantly placed himself well above the other disciples. *Lord, even if all these weak men walk away from Your side, I, Your strongest disciple, will never desert You.*

All this blustering self-assertion revealed a decided misunderstanding of the danger confronting him. He had underestimated his enemy, overblown his ability, and undervalued His Lord. He seemed blind to the fact that his puny humanity was no match for the devil and that without his Lord's intercession he was bound to get creamed.

Peter thought that he knew himself better than Jesus did, and consequently, turned a deaf ear toward the wise words of his Master. Sadly, his choice of insubordination over submission affected the others as well as himself. Since he was their leader and since he led forcefully, the other disciples predictably followed him into harm's way.

The Stumble: Self-indulgent Prayerlessness

J. C. Ryle captured the essence of Peter's failure that night when he said, "There is no degree of sin into which the greatest saint may not run if not upheld by the grace of God, and if they do not watch and pray."[2] When Peter tripped over his self-confident boldness, he lost sight of his need to watch and pray in dependence on the grace of his Father to keep him from falling. His *trip* caused him to *stumble* into self-indulgence and go directly to sleep instead of to prayer.

The disciples had left the upper room with their Master shortly before midnight and accompanied Him to a garden known as Gethsemane. The Gospel accounts give us the impression that they were completely oblivious to the unimaginable burden Jesus was bearing at that critical moment. As His appointed hour drew near, His awareness of the price He would pay for the sins of His own seemed to immensely intensify. Jesus, in His divine nature, understood the horror of sin to a depth that we never will. Living in the midst of sinful humanity for thirty-plus years must have been a sore trial for the God-Man, but the very idea of *becoming sin* on behalf of the elect was enough to unnerve Him.

"Becoming sin" meant *being* the one thing He absolutely abhorred. It meant becoming the vile object of God's righteous wrath. It meant separation from the Trinitarian Oneness in which He had existed from all eternity. It meant being truly alone — something that He had never experienced. Contemplating the horror that was descending upon Him would soon escalate into an unbearable agony which He could not have endured without angelic assistance.

The thing I find most amazing in the Gospel accounts of that night is that the men to whom He was closest appear downright indifferent to His increasing distress. Scripture gives no indication that they offered Jesus any care and concern during this very darkest of all dark nights of the soul.

Of course, Jesus knew that His much-needed support on this night wouldn't be coming from His weak disciples. He knew that, in certain crises, the only source of real help is direct communion with God through earnest prayer. Thus, when He took His three key disciples into the Garden with Him, it was not with the intent of leaning on them, but so that they could watch Him lean on the Father.

You see, He knew that these men were also facing a crisis that evening, one of which they were only vaguely aware. And He knew that they wouldn't handle it well. Jesus was well aware that Peter's self-confidence had infected them all with a complacency deadly to earnest prayer, and that their apathetic indifference to impending danger disposed them toward self-indulgence instead of self-discipline.

He knew that they needed to see the intensity of satanic attack, and how very weak human strength really is. He wanted to teach them, by His example, to seek strength from God instead of relying on self. He wanted them to recognize their great need to "pray without ceasing," because He knew that these three had to teach the others about dependence on prayer in the midst of a crisis.

Interestingly, the men seem to have learned what Jesus wanted to teach them, but not by alertly watching and heeding His good example. Rather, they learned by their *failure* to watch and pray. When Peter later wrote "Be of sober spirit, be on the alert. Your adversary, the devil, prowls about like a roaring lion, seeking someone to devour" (1 Peter 5:8), he was most assuredly speaking from painful experience.

Scripture tells us that although Jesus forthrightly told them, "My soul is deeply grieved, to the point of death; remain here and keep watch with Me" (Matthew 26:38), they nodded off. We then read that when Jesus returned to find them peacefully snoring, He admonished them with these words: "So, you men could not keep watch with Me for one hour? Keep watching and praying, that you may not enter into temptation; the spirit is willing, but the flesh is weak" (v. 41).

Matthew tells us that He spoke directly to Peter, perhaps to remind him of his position as leader of leaders and of his responsibility to set the standard for the rest of the group. Peter, however, failed to give heed to His Master's warning and slept peacefully on until Jesus shook him awake to announce: "Behold, the hour is at hand and the Son of Man is being betrayed into the hands of sinners. Arise, let us be going; behold the one who betrays Me is at hand!" (vv. 45-46).

In the moments that followed, Peter behaved just like a bold, self-confident man who had been self-indulgently sleeping instead of earnestly praying. Caught up in confusion, panic, and anger, he resorted to violence in his Lord's defense, then recoiled from the resulting rebuke and left Jesus to face the mob all alone.

I wonder if Peter recalled Jesus' prophecy as he hot-footed it out of the garden with the other disciples: "You will all fall away because of Me this night, for it is written, 'I will strike down the shepherd, and the sheep of the flock will be scattered'" (v. 31). If so, perhaps that is why he didn't run very far.

The Crash: Self-deluding Foolhardiness

Matthew tells us that although "all the disciples left Him and fled," Peter followed Him "at a distance as far as the courtyard of the high priest, and entered in, and sat down with the officers to see the outcome" (vv. 56, 58). Although it might seem, at first glance, that he was acting in courage motivated by love, his behavior could be more aptly described as self-deluding foolhardiness. Peter walked right into the enemy's camp and made himself comfortable. In the words of Psalm 1, he had placed himself in the "path of sinners" and settled down in the "seat of scoffers" where he would be highly vulnerable to the "counsel of the wicked." Keeping such company is spiritually dangerous, and Peter was far from prepared to handle that challenge.

Although he was no doubt alert to the physical danger of his surroundings and ready to fight his way out of the crowd if need be, Peter seemed unaware of the spiritual peril lurking around him. Consequently, he was quickly blindsided by a mere servant-girl. "You too were with Jesus the Galilean," she bluntly declared in the hearing of all. And Peter denied it before them all saying, "I do not know what you are talking about" (vv. 69-70). Then another girl said to the crowd, "This man was with Jesus of Nazareth." And Peter replied with an oath, "I do not know the man" (vv. 71-21).

I wonder if Peter was listening to what he was saying. Was he astounded to hear himself deny knowing the Man who had brought his wife's mother back from death's door...the Man who had saved him from drowning in the Sea of Galilee...the Man who had shown him the glory of His transfiguration...the Man who had said, "before a cock crows, you shall deny Me three times"? If so, did Peter caution himself, *Be careful, old man, that was strike two?*

Apparently not.

Only a little while later, some bystanders recognized him and commented, "Surely you too are one of them; for the way you talk gives you away." To this Peter began to curse and swear, "I do not know the man!" Luke tells us that before he had finished speaking, he heard a cock crow, then turned to see Jesus looking directly at him (22:60-61). At that moment his world completely disintegrated. Luke says "he went out and wept bitterly" (v. 62).

R. Kent Hughes says "something died inside Peter that night — Simon the natural man with all his self-assured presumption."[3] God allowed Peter to fall farther than most saints have fallen, but then He forgave him, restored him, and used him more mightily than most saints are used. Although Satan's temptation had been designed to destroy the foundation stone of Christ's church, God chose to use it instead as a strengthening agent. The foundation stone's failure purged him of weak self-assurance and taught him to lean wholly on Christ. Within a few years, Peter would admonish other tempted believers:

> *Humble yourselves, therefore, under the mighty hand of God, that He may exalt you at the proper time, casting all your anxiety upon Him, because He cares for you. Be of sober spirit, be on the alert. Your adversary, the devil, prowls about like a roaring lion, seeking someone to devour. But resist him, firm in your faith, knowing that the same experiences of suffering are being accomplished by your brethren who are in the world. And after you have suffered for a little while, the God of all grace, who called you to His eternal glory in Christ, will Himself perfect, confirm, strengthen, and establish you. To Him be dominion forever and ever. Amen.*
> (1 Peter 5:8-11)

Such words could have only been written by one who had lived them. I'm sure that Peter repented in recurrent floods of tearful grief, and I'm equally sure that God comforted him as he did so by bringing His Lord's gracious words often to mind: "when once you have turned again...let not your heart be troubled...strengthen your brothers...believe in

God, believe also in Me...I go to prepare a place for you...that where I am, there you may be also."

John MacArthur has said that "the single greatest gift God could conceivably give to mankind is forgiveness of sins."[4] Then he goes on to affirm that in the light of Peter's repentance and the Lord's gracious forgiveness, the story of Peter's tragic denial is extremely encouraging.[5] Although Peter's denial chills us with its warning to beware of relying on weak human flesh, his full restoration to service thrills us with the promise of God's super-abounding grace.

I think the foundation stone of Christ's church would shout *Amen!* to that.

Notes:

1. Alexander Maclaren, *Expositions of Holy Scriptures* (Grand Rapids, Mich.: Baker, 1871), 246, (referenced in R. Kent Hughes, *Preaching the Word: Luke, vol. 2, That You May Know the Truth* [Wheaton, Ill.: Crossway Books, 1998], 328.)

2. J. C. Ryle, *The Crossway Classic Commentaries: Luke*, series eds., Alister Mcgrath & J. I. Packer (Wheaton, Ill.: Crossway Books, 1993), 232.

3. R. Kent Hughes, *Preaching the Word: Luke, vol. 2, That You May Know the Truth* (Wheaton, Ill.: Crossway Books, 1998), 351.

4. John MacArthur Jr., *The MacArthur New Testament Commentary: Matthew 24-28* (Chicago: Moody Press, 1989), 211.

5. Ibid, 212.

Review Questions

1. In your own words, describe the glorious promise contained in Jesus' words to Peter found in Luke 22:31-32. Why do you think Jesus spoke these words to Peter *before* He told him that he would betray Him? How do Jesus' words in John 13:38-14:3 relate to this situation?

2. List and *briefly* describe the steps in Peter's great fall.

3. Explain how Peter's misplaced confidence revealed his misunderstanding of the danger confronting him. How did his behavior affect the other disciples?

4. Describe, in your own words, the horrible crisis Jesus experienced in the Garden of Gethsemane. How did the disciples react to His agony? How should they have behaved in the Garden with Jesus? Did they learn the lesson Jesus intended to teach them in spite of their behavior? Explain. What does this tell you about the accomplishment of God's sovereign purposes?

5. Relate Peter's "hanging out" in the courtyard of the high priest to Psalm 1. Be sure to include an explanation of how his denial of Jesus was facilitated by the self-deluding foolhardiness of his actions.

6. Read Psalm 130:1-6 and use it to explain how Peter's denial of Christ is both convicting and encouraging for all believers. How does this incident specifically convict and encourage you in your walk with the Lord?

Applying the Word

1. This week review the verses you have memorized from previous lessons. Then begin memorizing one or more of the following:

   Psalm 1:1-6
   John 14:1-3
   1 Peter 5:8-11

2. J. Glyn Owen, in his book *From Simon to Peter*, explains that Satan specifically targeted Peter because he would prove to be immensely useful to God and wield a great deal of spiritual influence. Satan does not waste his time, Owen remarks, on those who do not threaten his kingdom. Then Owen asks his readers, "Are you sufficiently menacing to the enemy's position that he should have an interest in you?" (J. Glyn Owen, *From Simon to Peter* [Welwyn, Herts, England: Evangelical Press, 1985], 205-211) Examine your heart and life prayerfully, and then answer Owen's question.

3. Have you experienced a crisis in which your only source of real help was direct communion with God through earnest prayer? If so, describe it. Did you have any support from other believers during this crisis? If so, explain why their support alone was insufficient to carry you through this crisis. How did enduring this crisis in deep dependence on God strengthen your faith? How has it equipped you to teach others about the great value of prayer?

4. Have you experienced a great fall similar to Peter's? If so, describe it. How did you respond to your great fall? Have you sensed God's cleansing forgiveness and full restoration to service? If so, describe the comfort you find in Jesus' words recorded in Luke 22:31-32 and in John 14:1-3. If not, seek counsel and help from your pastor, another of your church leaders, or a mature Christian mentor or friend.

Digging Deeper

1. A friend of mine once told me, "Before God can use a man (or a woman) greatly, He must break him (or her) greatly." Do you agree with my friend? Using what you have learned about Peter so far in this study, explain why or why not.

"Hark, my soul! it is the Lord;
'Tis the Savior, hear his word;
Jesus speaks, and speaks to thee;
'Say, poor sinner, lovest thou me?'...

"Lord, it is my chief complaint,
That my love is weak and faint;
Yet I love thee and adore.
Oh, for grace to love thee more!"

William Cowper

Chapter 11

The Thrill of Forgiveness

(Bible reading: Isaiah 53; Matthew 28:1-10; Mark 16:1-8; Luke 23:50-24:12; John 19:38-21:23; 1 Corinthians 15:3-5)

Scripture mercifully draws a thick curtain around Simon Peter from the time of his denial until Christ's resurrection, and allows the wretched disciple to agonize privately. I imagine that he spent most of that time without human companionship, learning by hard experience the lesson he self-assuredly slept through in the garden with Jesus. The time Peter spent in grievous repentance was surely one of those crises that can be endured only through earnest, prayerful communion with God the Father. The three days that his Lord lay dead in the tomb must have been Peter's own private Gethsemane.

Did Peter eventually seek solace from the other disciples? Did they compassionately come looking for him? We have no way of knowing, but we do know that they finally regrouped and went into hiding. And we can assume that, to a man, they were frightened, grief-stricken, and deeply ashamed of their behavior toward Jesus.

I find it quite interesting that while the Lord's leaders were hiding, some of His followers were acting quite boldly. Two secret disciples, whose fear of man had previously rendered them testimonially mute, bravely approached Pontius Pilate to claim Jesus' body. This act took courage not only because it jeopardized their positions with the Sanhedrin, but also because it openly aligned them with One convicted and executed for the crime of sedition. Rome typically handed the bodies of criminals over to next of kin, unless they had been crucified as seditionists. Those bodies bore the ultimate shame and indignity of being left as prey for vultures and predators.[1]

Pilate honored Joseph of Arimathea's request, perhaps because he believed that Jesus was innocent, or perhaps simply to flout Jewish authority, but surely in unwitting accord with God's divine providence. If Jesus' body had not been rescued from its "assigned" place with the wicked and laid to rest "with a rich man" because of His innocence, Isaiah's prophecy would have gone unfulfilled (53:9).

Nicodemus, who had first come to Jesus by night, brought spices and helped Joseph prepare Jesus' body for burial, and together they laid Him in Joseph's new tomb. Then they retired, perhaps in the company of other sorrowful followers, to quietly "celebrate" the bleakest of Passovers any had known.

Also included among Jesus' bold, active followers was a committed group of indomitable ladies. Scripture tells us that they were up before dawn on the first day of the week to make their way to the tomb in which Jesus was buried. The women, (Mary Magdalene, Mary the wife of Clopas, Salome, and Joanna) carried more spices to anoint the body of Jesus and complete the process of burial. They were concerned about how they were going to get into the tomb since even their combined physical strength would be no match for the stone that sealed its entrance.

I have always admired these gutsy ladies whose great love for the Lord empowered their undertaking a task beyond their abilities. J. C. Ryle seemed to have admired them also. He says that all Christians could learn a much-needed lesson from their example: "Let us pray for more practical faith. Let us believe that in the path of duty, we shall never be entirely deserted. Let us go forward boldly, and we shall often find that the lion in the way is chained, and what seems a hedge of thorns is only a shadow." [2]

As first light illumined the tomb of their Lord, those dedicated first-century ladies were blessed to discover that God graciously meets every need of His servants who boldly follow the path He has laid out before them.

Jesus Has Left the Tomb

As they approached the tomb, the women were stunned to see the great stone rolled away from the entrance and a man whose "appearance was like lightning and his garment as white as snow" sitting upon it. John MacArthur aptly remarks that obviously the stone had not been removed to let Jesus out, but to let His people in![3]

Scripture tells us that Mary Magdalene (who may well have been the youngest and fleetest) took one look and ran off to fetch the disciples. Clearly, she knew where they were hiding and probably shocked them by bursting in and exclaiming, "They have taken away the Lord out of the tomb, and we do not know where they have laid Him" (John 20:1-2). It was still early morning and the disciples may have been barely awake. Luke indicates that her words "appeared to them as nonsense" and they refused to believe her (24:11). However, Peter and John seemed to sense her sincerity and took off to investigate.

Meanwhile back at the tomb, the other women were hearing an astounding announcement. Jesus was no longer there. In fact, He was no longer dead. He had risen just as He told them He would. They were to come in and see where He had been lying, and then quickly go and tell the disciples, *particularly Peter*, that He had risen and was going before them into Galilee. Each time I read Mark's account of the angel's instructions, I am deeply touched by his mention of Peter. Surely, these words reflect the Lord's deep concern for His anguished disciple and His intense desire to see him fully restored.

The amazed ladies obeyed the angel immediately and "with fear and great joy" departed to tell the disciples what they had experienced. Then to their even greater amazement, Jesus met them on the way, received their worship, and graciously reassured them that they had indeed been chosen to bear first witness of His resurrection (Matthew 28:8-9). What a great blessing for those faithful women! In their culture the testimony of women was routinely discarded as unreliable, and yet the risen Lord of the Universe was entrusting first proclamation of this most significant testimony to female voices.

Apparently, in their rush to tell the disciples, they failed to cross paths with Peter and John. Scripture indicates that when the two men arrived at the tomb, it was deserted. John had outrun "the big fisherman," arrived first, and slowed down to cautiously peer into the entrance. In a matter of moments however, Peter, in characteristic exuberance, flew at full speed right past him into the *not quite empty* tomb.

The grave clothes, strips of linen fabric, were lying in place, as they had been when wrapped around Jesus, but flattened by at least seventy-five pounds of burial spices. The separate face cloth which had covered His head was "rolled up in a place by itself" (John 20:6-7). Although Peter's body had screeched to a halt inside the tomb, his mind was most likely still racing full tilt. I can just picture him rubbing his forehead and puzzling, *What happened here? Obviously, Mary Magdalene's theory was wrong. Jesus' body hasn't been stolen. No grave robber would have (or could have) taken the body and left the wrappings looking like that. But if no one stole the body, where did it go?*

William Hendriksen remarks in his commentary on John that Peter usually acted before John did, whereas John usually understood before Peter did.[4] And such was the case at this climactic moment. Perhaps emboldened by Peter's presence, John followed his friend into the tomb. Scripture tells us that he took one look at the grave clothes and knew immediately what had happened to Jesus. In his own words, he tells us, "So the other disciple who had first come to the tomb entered then also, and he saw and believed" (v. 8).

What was it that he saw and believed? William Hendriksen sums it up well: "What did he see? Exactly what Peter had seen. What did he believe? That Jesus was actually risen from the dead, and was the real Messiah, the Lord of Glory, the Son of God in the most exalted sense. This is nothing less than living faith in the act of embracing the truth of the resurrection."[5]

Although Scripture indicates fairly clearly that Peter's understanding of the resurrection lagged behind John's, it doesn't tell us specifically when he first saw the light. I tend to think that John worked hard at explaining his own understanding, but that Peter did not really get it until he saw his risen Lord face to face. Paul tells us in 1 Corinthians 15:5 that Jesus met with Peter privately, most likely before He appeared to the other disciples; however, nowhere in Scripture do we have any record of what transpired at that crucial meeting.

Wouldn't you love to know what they said to each other? I certainly would. But on the other hand, I'm glad to see that this intensely personal moment between Peter and Jesus has been marked "Confidential." God's Holy Spirit determined that the details surrounding that pregnant encounter would remain a matter of their private concern. Peter was blessed to express His repentance and receive full forgiveness within the shelter of Jesus' "covering" love.

Apparently, Peter never forgot the warmth of that shelter. Years later, he encouraged scattered believers, *"above all, keep fervent in your love for one another, because love covers a multitude of sins"* (1 Peter 5:8). In a culture that revels in "full exposure," we need this reminder that love deals with sin as discreetly as possible.

Discipleship Lessons in Galilee

After the private meeting with Peter, Jesus appeared at least twice to the disciples in Jerusalem (John 20:19-29) before instructing them to meet Him in Galilee. Seeing their Lord alive, touching His wounds, and hearing His words from the other side of the grave changed them immeasurably. They were experiencing things that could not be explained apart from God's direct intervention in their affairs. The strength of the testimony they would eventually bear to the world grew out of this fact. As C. T. Craig has expressed it, they "did not believe in the resurrection of Christ because they could not find his body; they believed because they did find a living Christ."[6]

Jesus may have chosen to meet them in Galilee simply because it was quieter there. His final days with them on earth would be brief and momentous. Perhaps He desired to spend them in a setting far less distracting than bustling Jerusalem. He may also have told His disciples, out of concern for their safety, not to travel together in one large group. That would explain why only seven of them were present when He manifested Himself at the Sea of Tiberias.

Peter had joined Thomas, Nathaniel, James, John, and two unnamed disciples on the shore and must have quickly grown restless. "I am going fishing," he said, to which the others responded, "We will come with you" (John 21:2-3). Some scholars read Peter's announcement as an open rejection of Christ. His return to fishing, they say, expressed his intent to forsake discipleship and pursue his old business.

Other scholars, with whom I tend to agree, think Peter's action was motivated more by industriousness than by desertion. Peter was not given to sitting around, and may well have been pacing the shore within five or ten minutes of his arrival! Scripture gives us no reason to think that Peter was on the brink of apostasy. He had seen Jesus at least three times, once in private and twice with the other disciples, and was clearly eager to see Him again. If Peter had been thinking desertion, it seems highly unlikely that he would have thrown himself in the water and raced to meet Jesus as soon as John identified Him in the dawn's early light.

But did Peter's industriousness necessarily make this decision a good one? James Montgomery Boice argues convincingly that it did not. He describes Peter's fishing trip as the first of several essential discipleship lessons Jesus taught him that day.[7] Although Peter had been forgiven and restored to full fellowship with his Lord and Savior, he wasn't yet ready to assume the leadership role prepared for him in eternity past. Before he could lead the first-century Church, he needed equipping. That equipping would come in two distinct stages, the first taking the form of several discipleship lessons taught on the shore of the Sea of Tiberius, and the second descending upon him and the others at Pentecost in Jerusalem.

Jesus may well have deliberately kept the disciples waiting for Him in Galilee to set the stage for Peter's first lesson. The fisherman was both energetic and extremely impatient, a combination that inclined him toward impetuosity. By ordering the outcome of Peter's impulsive fishing trip on Tiberius, Jesus taught him a valuable discipleship lesson: *Although it is possible to sincerely serve Him in the energy of the flesh, such self-designed efforts always prove fruitless.* Before Christian work will be blessed, it must be undertaken in obedience to Christ's direction. Waiting for direction must have been a hard lesson for Peter to learn, just as it is for all enthusiastic disciples. However, we know that he did, in fact, learn it. In Acts 1, we find him patiently waiting with other believers for the descent of the Spirit, in complete submission to his Lord's instructions.

Jesus also prepared breakfast for Peter and his companions that day, teaching him to rely upon divine provision of need. Significantly, Jesus had fish and bread cooking on a charcoal fire *before* the men's catch was hauled ashore. He did, however, invite them to contribute part of what they had caught. The lesson is clear: *Jesus does not need our efforts to get His work done, although He graciously uses our obedience to work out His purposes.*

When the group had finished eating, Jesus asked Peter pointblank, "Simon, son of John, do you love me more than these?" (John 21:15). Interpreting what He meant by that question presents us with a challenge because the word "these" is downright ambiguous. Was He asking Peter if he loved Him more than he loved fishing? Or if he loved Him more than he loved the other disciples? Or was He asking whether Peter still thought he loved Him more than the other disciples loved Him?

I lean toward the last option because it would have reminded them all of Peter's proud boast, "Even though all may fall away because of You, I will never fall away" (Matthew 26:33). Just a short time before, Peter had indeed claimed to love Jesus more than did the others; but in the ensuing days, his attitude underwent a radical transformation. Now, he eschewed his former self-confidence and appealed to Jesus' perfect knowledge of his repentant heart. "Yes, Lord; You know that I love you." Jesus may well have nodded assent before responding with this clear directive: "Tend My lambs."

Jesus then asked Peter the same question twice more, received essentially the same answer, and repeated the same directive. John tells us that Peter was grieved by the third question but does not tell us why. Some scholars suggest that his grief sprang from the Lord's shift from *agapao* (the Greek word for love always used in relationship to God) in the first two questions to *phileo* (the Greek word for human love expressing itself in friendship) in the final question. However, other scholars downplay that distinction by explaining that John often used these two words interchangeably.

In either case, I am inclined to believe that Peter grieved because Jesus' thrice repeated question reminded him of his thrice-repeated denial. Since Peter loved Jesus wholeheartedly, remembering his fall had to have been painful. However, Jesus appeared to be urging Peter not to get bogged down in grief. He had been forgiven and fully restored to His Master. It was no longer appropriate for Peter's great love for Jesus to be expressed in grief. It was time to move on. Just as that love had motivated gut-wrenching repentance, it should now stimulate Christ-exalting service.

"Tend My sheep," Jesus told him in the presence of all the disciples, officially commissioning him to the task God prepared for him before time began. Then He explained where that task would eventually lead him. "Truly, truly, I say to you, when you were younger, you used to gird yourself, and walk wherever you wished; but when you grow old, you will stretch out your hands, and someone else will gird you, and bring you where you do not wish to go" (John 21:17-18). Perhaps Jesus gave Peter a moment to ponder this graphic depiction of the kind of death by which he would glorify God before He added this watershed order: "Follow Me."

Here is another essential discipleship lesson. *Those who follow Jesus must accept restrictions of their individual liberty and give undivided attention to duty.* A. B. Bruce, in his book *The Training of the Twelve*, elaborates, "He who has a Christian heart must feel that he is strong and wise for the sake of others who want strength and wisdom; and he will undertake the shepherd's office, though shrinking with fear and trembling from its responsibilities, and though conscious also that in so doing he is consenting to have his liberty and independence greatly circumscribed."[8]

Peter seemed to have counted the cost of discipleship and found it a bargain, but he had a question. Turning around and pointing toward John, he asked Jesus, "Lord, and what about this man?" (v. 21).

"If I want him to remain until I come, what is that to you?" Jesus shot back. "You follow Me!" The final discipleship lesson Jesus taught Peter that day may well have been the hardest to swallow: *God doesn't treat all disciples alike.* John Calvin explained it like this, "God may choose just one person in ten to test with weighty calamities or with massive labors, and he might allow the other nine to remain in their ease, or at least test them only lightly. In any case, God does not treat everyone in the same way but tests everyone as he thinks suitable."[9]

John doesn't tell us how Peter reacted to Jesus' final discipleship lesson. Did he shrug his shoulders and quip, "OK, whatever."? Did he slap his forehead and say, "Of course, you're right. What was I thinking?" Or did he bite his tongue, swallow hard, and think, "Man, that seems so unfair!"? My money's on option three.

Most of us tend to bristle when our sense of fairness is violated — even when the One doing the violating is God Almighty. We have a hard time remembering that God's ways are not our ways, and that His doesn't define "fair" the same way that we do. God doesn't distribute hardship and blessing as evenly as we would like, because He has designed and equipped each one of us for differing ministries. Discipleship challenges us, just as it did Peter, to follow Christ without looking around to see where other disciples are going.

Notes:

1. D. A. Carson, *The Pillar New Testament Commentary: The Gospel According to John* (Grand Rapids, Mich.: William B. Eerdmans Publishing Company, 1991), 629.

2. J. C. Ryle, *The Crossway Classic Commentaries: Mark,* Series eds., Alister McGrath and J. I. Packer (Wheaton, Ill.: Crossway Books, 1993), 261.

3. John MacArthur Jr., *The MacArthur New Testament Commentary: Matthew 24-28* (Chicago: Moody Press, 1989), 309.

4. William Hendriksen, *New Testament Commentary: John* (Grand Rapids, Mich.: Baker Book House, 1953), 479.

5. Ibid, 451.

6. C. T. Craig, *The Beginning of Christianity* (New York/ Nashville, 1943), 135. Quoted in F. F. Bruce, *The Gospel of John* (Grand Rapids, Mich.: William B. Eerdmans Publishing Company, 1983), 386.

7. James Montgomery Boice, *The Gospel of John, vol. 4: Triumph Through Tragedy: John 18-21* (Grand Rapids, Mich.: Baker Book House, 1985, 1999), 1624ff.

8. A. B. Bruce, *The Training of the Twelve* (Grand Rapids, Mich.: Kregel Publications, 1971, 1988), 522

9. John Calvin, *The Crossway Classic Commentaries: John,* Series eds., Alister McGrath and J. I. Packer (Wheaton, Ill.: Crossway Books, 1994), 471.

Review Questions

1. Do you believe that "the days that his Lord lay dead in the
    tomb must have been Peter's own private Gethsemane"?
    Drawing upon what you have learned about Simon
    Peter so far in this study, explain in your own words
    what you think he may have been thinking and feeling
    during that time.

2. Two significant time periods in Peter's life are heavily
    veiled in Scripture: the time between the crucifixion
    and the resurrection, and Jesus' private meeting with
    him after the resurrection. The Holy Spirit has revealed
    nothing to us about those crucial periods in Peter's life.
    However, Peter may have been alluding to them when
    he wrote 1 Peter 4:8. Read 1 Peter 4:8 in the light of
    these "covered" periods in Peter's life, and explain what
    you learn about Christ's love for Peter. How should we
    follow Christ's example in loving others?

3. Describe the behavior of Joseph of Arimathea, Nicode-
    mus, Mary Magdalene, Mary the wife of Clopas, Salome,
    and Joanna after the crucifixion of Jesus while the
    disciples were in hiding. Do you believe these followers
    acted boldly and courageously? Why or why not?

4. Read John 20:1-10 and consult reputable commentaries
    regarding these verses. Then explain what John saw in the
    tomb that caused him to believe. According to William
    Hendriksen (see p. ____), what did John believe at that
    moment? To what do you attribute Peter's slowness to
    believe what John apparently believed immediately?
    What do these two men's reactions to the empty tomb

tell you about the way God's Holy Spirit illumines the minds of His children?

5. List the discipleship lessons Jesus taught Peter at the Sea of Tiberius in Galilee. Then describe in your own words, the significance of each of these lessons.

6. Read John 21:1-23, focusing particularly on the behavior of Peter. What evidence do you see that his basic attitude has been radically transformed? To what do you attribute this transformation? What aspects of Peter's character appear less radically transformed and still in need of work? Relate these aspects of Peter's character to the discipleship lessons Jesus taught him. Why was it important for Peter to learn these lessons well?

Applying the Word

1. This week review the verses you have memorized from previous lessons. Then begin memorizing one or more of the following:

   1 Corinthians 15:3-5
   1 Peter 4:8
   1 Peter 4:19

2. J. C. Ryle praised the exemplary behavior of the women who went to Christ's tomb with these words: "Let us pray for more practical faith. Let us believe that in the path of duty, we shall never be entirely deserted. Let us go forward boldly, and we shall often find that the lion in the way is chained, and what seems a hedge of thorns is only a shadow."[2] When the women left home on that first-century morning, they were embarking upon a ministry that was clearly beyond their own abilities, and yet they proceeded without hesitation. Although they were concerned about the seemingly insurmountable obstacles in their path of duty, they didn't wait for the path to be perfectly clear before they began. Are you like those women? Do you typically proceed in the way God has called you even when you look down the road and see lions and thorn hedges barring your path? Or do you routinely wait for clear paths before stepping out into ministry? Cite several examples from your experience to support your assessment of your customary behavior. If you are not like these women, determine what is hindering you from imitating their boldness and begin making changes in your life that will help you walk in their footprints. If necessary, seek help from your pastor, another of your church leaders, or a mature Christian mentor or friend.

3. Write out each of the discipleship lessons Jesus taught Peter at the Sea of Tiberius in Galilee, leaving three or four inches of space between them. In those spaces, list examples from your customary behavior that indicate how well or how poorly you have learned each of those lessons. Which lessons have you learned well? Which have you learned poorly? What do you need to do in order to improve in those areas in which you have learned poorly? Make a specific step by step plan that will help you improve in those areas. Who do you know who loves you enough to encourage you to faithfully carry out your plan and to hold you accountable? When will you ask that person to help you? How might you help others to learn the lessons that you have learned well?

Digging Deeper

1. Scripture indicates that Nicodemus and Joseph of Arimathea were secret disciples "for fear of the Jews" (John 19:38-39) until after Jesus was crucified. What was it, do you think, about the crucifixion that canceled their fear of man and made them open disciples? (Suggestion: Reading Ed Welch's book, *When People are Big and God is Small*, may help you formulate some thoughts in answering this question.)

"Pentecost was a new creation."

ॐ

Dennis E. Johnson

Chapter 12

Upon This Rock

(Bible reading: Acts 1:1-2:42; 3:1-4:37; 5:1-42; 9:32-11:18; 12:1-19; 2 Corinthians 5:17; 1 Peter 5:6-7)

The Peter we see in the opening chapters of Acts had come a long way since his first encounter with Jesus. The fisher of men who stepped up to lead Christ's fledgling Church bore little resemblance to the fisher of fish who had heard Andrew announce, "We have found the Messiah!" Three years with Jesus had changed him immeasurably. The self-sufficient, self-confident, self-assertive disciple had been humbled by God — and consequently had learned to humble himself. Learning that lesson well gained him the blessing of being exalted by God to a key leadership role in the first century church (1 Peter 5:6-7). The rock upon which the New Covenant Church would be built had finally solidified.

Peter had become a "new creation in Christ." His old self-assurance had "passed away," and a new Christ-dependence had taken its place (2 Corinthians 5:17). Self-centered Simon had been crucified with Christ and no longer lived. Christ-centered Peter had been raised to walk in newness of life. The life he now lived in the flesh, he lived by faith in the Son of God who had loved him and delivered Himself up for him (Romans 6:3-5; Galatians 2:20).

As we take a brief look at Peter in Acts, we won't be able to miss the radical change in his life. We'll see a man who now took every thought, action, and attitude captive to the obedience of Christ (2 Corinthians 10:5). We'll see a man who now seized each new day confident in the knowledge that whether he lived or died, he was the Lord's (Romans 14:7-9). We'll see a man whose great gifts and abilities were now exercised in submission to God's Holy Spirit. In short, we'll see a living example of what Dennis Johnson has called the new creation of Pentecost.[1]

There is only one way to explain Peter's distinct transformation. He and the other disciples "received power" when the Holy Spirit was poured out upon them at Pentecost. Jesus Christ had ascended to the right hand of God where He received from His Father the promised Spirit to pour out on His people (Acts 2:33). His action granted Moses's heartfelt desire that "all the Lord's people...would...[have] His Spirit upon them" (Numbers 11:29), and fulfilled Ezekiel's Old Covenant prophecy: "I will put My Spirit within you and cause you to walk in My statutes, and you will be careful to observe My ordinances" (36:27).

Pentecost was a "new creation" because God's Holy Spirit had finally come to indwell and empower each and every believer in Christ. What an incredible blessing! Those who have been redeemed from the power of sin by the atonement of Christ can be transformed just as radically as was Simon Peter. All we need do is walk in the footprints of his willing submission to God's Holy Spirit.

Salvation in Christ "baptizes" us by His Spirit into one body, unites us with Christ, and empowers us to obey His commands (1 Corinthians 12:13; Romans 6:5, 17-18). However, submitting to His control requires effort on our part. Although Paul emphasized that all those who belong to Christ have His Holy Spirit dwelling within them (Romans 8:9), he also admonished believers to continually "be filled with the Spirit" (Ephesians 5:18) and to avoid grieving or quenching Him (Ephesians 4:30; 1 Thessalonians 5:19).

Obviously, having God's Spirit within us doesn't wipe out our wills. We can be born of the Spirit and not be filled with His power when we choose to resist Him. Such behavior amounts to rebellion against our Lord Jesus Christ and tragically cripples our worthy walk in His service. Paul commands us to "be filled with the Spirit" because he knows how quickly and easily we slip into rebellion, but he also assures us that God's Holy Spirit does more than simply demand our obedience. He also empowers it.

Peter's willing submission to God's Holy Spirit bears eloquent testimony to that same Spirit's working within him to enable obedience. As we examine the newly created Peter, we'll see him reflect the Spirit's transforming power in telling displays of newly created courage, newly created wisdom, and newly created contentment.

Newly Created Courage

Perhaps the clearest mark of the Holy Spirit's transforming work in believers is the retooling and redirection of their natural abilities. As Christians begin to submit to the Spirit's control, their God-given talents and skills are honed for the purpose of pursuing God's kingdom and righteousness. Of course, God's Spirit also imbues believers with new graces and gifts, but His work of restructuring old inclinations can be much more dramatic. The remarkable changes we see in post-Pentecost Peter are a clear case in point.

Peter may well have been born bold and outspoken. The Gospels portray him as a man who often acted on impulse and spoke without thinking. Thus far in our study, we have seen how these traits were often spurred by self-interest and thus got him in trouble. Now as we turn our attention to the portrait of Peter painted in Acts, we'll see a man who, although still bold and outspoken, was no longer in trouble. That's because God's Holy Spirit had established His residence in Peter's heart, transforming his self-centered assertiveness into God-honoring courage.

On the very day that the Lord Jesus poured forth the Spirit, the man who had self-protectively denied knowing his Lord stood up and preached a bold Christ-centered sermon. He explained to the huge multinational crowd that the wonders about which they were so curious had, in fact, inaugurated "the last days" of Joel's ancient prophecy. He proclaimed that the Nazarene, Jesus, was their Messiah, that He was the One of whom David had spoken, and that they were responsible for His death on the cross.

"Therefore let all the house of Israel know for certain that God has made Him both Lord and Christ — this Jesus whom you crucified," he affirmed in summation, piercing to the heart his guilt-ridden audience. "Brethren, what shall we do?" they asked Peter, who forthrightly responded: "Repent, and let each of you be baptized in the name of

Jesus Christ for the forgiveness of your sins; and you shall receive the gift of the Holy Spirit. For the promise is for you and your children, and for all who are far off, as many as the Lord our God shall call to Himself" (Acts 2:36-39).

Luke tells us that "with many other words he solemnly testified and kept on exhorting them, saying, 'Be saved from this perverse generation!'" (v. 40). Edward Donnelly commented on Peter's preaching by saying, "Again and again he plunges the sword of the Spirit up to the hilt in the consciences of his hearers" and that "he is direct not only in preaching sin but in preaching grace."[2] That Peter could move from bold, outspoken denial to such powerful preaching within a few weeks bears startling testimony to the Spirit's transforming work in his life.

Peter's newly created God-honoring courage was not only reflected in his bold, outspoken preaching, but also in the way that he handled his enemies. Twice he was hauled before Jewish officials who were outraged by his preaching and concomitant working of attesting miracles (3:1-4:22; 5:12-32). Although he was threatened, beaten, and thrown into prison, Peter consistently defended the Lord instead of himself.

"Whether it is right in the sight of God to give heed to you rather than God, you be the judge; for we cannot stop speaking what we have seen and heard" (4:19-20), he proclaimed on one occasion. And shortly thereafter, he was equally firm: "We must obey God rather than men. The God of our fathers raised up Jesus, whom you had put to death by hanging Him on a cross. He is the one whom God exalted to His right hand as a Prince and a Savior, to grant repentance to Israel, and forgiveness of sins. And we are witnesses of these things; and so is the Holy Spirit, whom God has given to those who obey Him" (5:29-32).

The Peter we see standing firm in the face of grave danger had come a long way from the man who had high-tailed it out of Gethsemane and gone into hiding somewhere in Jerusalem. And it appears that his newly created courage was stimulated by some newly created habits of God-centered praying. Scripture provides us with no indication that the disciples prayed very well before receiving the Spirit. In fact, we see in the Gospels that they were inclined toward sleeping when they should have been praying! But after God's Spirit descended, we see them praying for confidence to proclaim God's Gospel boldly even in the midst of perilous opposition (Acts 4:23-30).

The book of Acts tells us that God answered this prayer when "the place where they had gathered together was shaken, and they were all filled with the Holy Spirit, and began to speak the word of God with boldness" (v. 31). Post-Pentecost Peter did not run away from hazardous threats to his personal safety, but joined the other disciples in "rejoicing that they had been considered worthy to suffer shame for His name. And every day, in the temple and from house to house, they kept right on teaching and preaching Jesus as the Christ" (5:41-42). We would be hard pressed to find a more stunning example of the Spirit's retooling and redirection of these recreated disciples.

Newly Created Wisdom

The pouring forth of the Spirit at Pentecost not only infused Peter with newly created boldness, it also filled him to the brim with newly created wisdom. We might say that the coming of God's Holy Spirit transformed a "wise guy" into a truly wise man. The primary difference I see between wise guys and wise men is the direction and extent of their typical mindset.

Wise guys are self-centered and clearly shortsighted. They tend to speak quickly and to base their remarks on the way that a particular circumstance has affected them personally. Truly wise men, on the other hand, think with a longer and broader perspective. They consider events in the light of the past and the future, gather all the relevant information they can, and then use what they've learned to make sense of circumstances. Wise men don't talk as much as do wise guys, but when they do speak, what they say is worth hearing.

The Peter we saw in the Gospels, although unabashedly committed to Christ, was also self-centered and clearly shortsighted. The man who spoke quickly to rebuke His Lord and to recommend building mountain-top tabernacles was assessing circumstances wholly on the basis of their affect upon him. Pre-Pentecost Peter lacked the wisdom of a God-centered perspective. His shortsighted perception of the events of his life didn't include understanding of God's purposes for them. Therefore, he reacted to them more like a wise guy than a wise man.

The descent of the Holy Spirit upon him, however, changed all of that. The indwelling Spirit brought divine insight to Peter, shifting his focus to God and expanding his perspective of human events. The Peter we see in Acts had been equipped by the Spirit to look wisely at life through God-colored glasses.

One place in which we see Peter's newly created wisdom starkly displayed is in his riveting preaching. In each of Peter's recorded sermons in Acts (2:14-40; 3:12-26; 4:8-12; 10:28-43), he captivated his listeners by first addressing events and ideas about which they were concerned and then deftly using those very concerns to confront them with their sin and introduce them to Christ.

He informed curious spectators (and speculators) who were intrigued by the signs and wonders accompanying the outpouring of the Spirit: "These men are not drunk, as you suppose,...but this is what was spoken of through the prophet Joel....Men of Israel, listen to these words: Jesus the Nazarene, a man attested to you by God with miracles and wonders and signs which God performed through Him in your midst, just as you yourselves know — this Man, delivered up by the predetermined plan and foreknowledge of God, you nailed to a cross by the hands of godless men and put Him to death" (2:15-16, 22-23).

He told the crowd gathering around the healed beggar at the Beautiful Gate of the Temple: "Why do you marvel at this, or why do you gaze at us, as if by our own power or piety we had made him walk? The God of Abraham, Isaac, and Jacob, the God of our fathers, has glorified His servant Jesus, the one whom you delivered up, and disowned in the presence of Pilate, when he had decided to release Him" (3:12-13).

He confronted the antagonistic Jewish Council with, "Rulers and elders of the people, if we are on trial today for a benefit done to a sick man, as to how this man has been made well, let it be known to all of you, and to all the people of Israel, that by the name of Jesus Christ the Nazarene, whom you crucified, whom God raised from the dead — by this name this man stands here before you in good health" (4:8-10). And he assured an assembly of God-fearing Gentiles, "I most certainly understand now that God is not one to show partiality, but in every nation the man who fears Him and does what is right, is welcome to come to Him" (10:34-35).

Peter's preaching was wise because of its eternal perspective and God-centered relevance. The Holy Spirit had blessed him with insight regarding the hearts of the lost and then led him to structure his preaching so as to attract their attention. Since depraved sinners have lost all natural taste for God's truth, wise preachers carefully season their sermons to whet fallen appetites. And one of the very best Gospel appetite stimulants is the enticing aroma of undeniable relevance. Peter made the mouths of lost sinners water by wisely leading them from the ephemeral relevance of their worldly concerns to the eternal relevance of salvation in Christ. In the words of Edward Donnelly, wise preaching like Peter's reveals to lost sinners that "in the light of sin and judgment, heaven and hell, their whole course of life is a tragic irrelevancy."[3]

Peter's newly created wisdom was also revealed in his God-centered responses to two stunning insights given him by the Spirit. In Acts 5, we see Peter discerning the lie of church members, Ananias and Sapphira, as well as the devil's foul purpose standing behind it. Recognizing the need to decisively foil this satanic first-strike at the church from within its own ranks, Peter forthrightly announced

God's fatal judgment upon the conspiratorial couple (Acts 5:4-5, 9).

Then in Acts 10, we watch Peter turn his life-long belief system completely around in response to God's word. After receiving an unarguable thrice-emphasized vision commanding him to dismantle traditionally cherished racial barriers, Peter accompanied a group of God-fearing Gentiles to the home of Cornelius. There he proclaimed the Gospel free of Jewish constraints and watched in amazement as God's Spirit was poured out upon them just as it had been at Pentecost. Then he returned to Jerusalem where he convinced those who "took issue with him" that "God has granted to the Gentiles also the repentance that leads to life" (11:2, 18).

Peter's behavior in these situations tells us that wisdom involves a lot more than merely receiving insight from God's Holy Spirit. It also requires acting upon it in ways that are God-centered and consistent with an eternal perspective. It requires responding to the Holy Spirit's enlightenment like a truly wise man instead of like a wise guy.

Newly Created Contentment

The outpouring of God's Holy Spirit at Pentecost also blessed Peter with newly created contentment. If you're like me, you struggle routinely to live in contentment. You understand that in Christ you should be content. You know that in Him you have all that you need for life and godliness. You believe that God loves you and that He will keep all His promises to you. And yet, you would like your life to be different. *If only your husband (wife, child, mother, father, sister, brother, boss, best friend) would come to know Christ....If only the "bad-influence family" next door would move out of state....If only your pastor could preach like the guys on the radio....If only your paycheck was a little bit bigger....If only the car would quit breaking down....If only....If only....*

We all struggle routinely to live in contentment because contentment is unnatural to fallen humanity. Paul tells us that contentment is something that we have to learn — and then he goes on to explain how we have to learn it:

> *But I rejoiced in the Lord greatly, that now at last you have revived your concern for me; indeed, you were concerned before, but you lacked opportunity. Not that I speak from want; for I have learned to be content in whatever circumstance I am. I know how to get along with humble means, and I also know how to live in prosperity; in any and every circumstance I have learned the secret of being filled and going hungry, both of having abundance and suffering need. I can do all things through Him who strengthens me.*
> (Philippians 4:10-13).

According to Paul, we learn contentment by looking to God for the strength to live well in any and every circumstance. Learning contentment involves recognizing that every situation of life has been ordained by God to serve as an arena in which to glorify Him, and that the precious gift of His Spirit equips us to respond to our circumstances in joyful submission. Peter's example in Acts is convicting for me, because he, like Paul, had learned "the secret of...suffering need," something that I am still a long way from grasping.

In Acts 12 we find Peter imprisoned once more, but this time his circumstances seemed particularly dire. Herod Agrippa I, a thoroughly unpleasant pagan, was on a rampage against Christians. Determined to hold on to his Jewish domain by ingratiating himself to the Jewish elite, he had launched a vicious attack against Jesus Christ's church. He killed James, the brother of John, with a sword; and when he saw that his death pleased the Jews, he arrested Peter and threw him in prison. As soon as Passover had ended, Herod would offer him up as the next bloody sacrifice to Jewish goodwill.

Frankly, if I had been in Peter's position, I would have been pretty bummed. I would have been grief-stricken over the cruel death of my friend and scared out of my wits at the quite-likely prospect of meeting the same kind of end. I would have been questioning God's love with one breath and pleading for rescue with the very next. I would have been an emotional basket-case, succumbing to panic, despair, and utter frustration. The one thing I would *not* have been is content.

However, *content* describes Peter perfectly. The man simply curled up between two burly soldiers and fell asleep! He had every reason to think he was facing a horrible death, and he had no reason to think he would be rescued again — and yet Peter slept soundly. So soundly in fact, that when a rescuer-angel did appear suddenly flooding his cell with bright light, Peter continued to peacefully snore. Luke tells us the angel had to strike his side in order to wake him up! Even then Peter was so groggy that he had to be told to get up, gird himself, put on his sandals, wrap his cloak around himself, and follow the angel out of the prison. Not until he was left alone in the street did he come to his senses and realize that he hadn't been dreaming.

Peter made his way to the home of John Mark's mother Mary, where the church had gathered to pray for him. We don't know exactly for what they were praying, but we do know that they didn't expect him to show up at the door! The servant girl, Rhoda, was so shocked when she saw him that she left him standing outside while she argued with the others about whether the man cooling his heels on the porch was really their leader. Peter, persistent as always, continued to knock until they let him in.

Peter described what had happened to him, told them to "report these things to James and the brethren," and then almost entirely dropped out of Acts. We'll see him only once more in this book at the Jerusalem Council.

Peter's almost-final exit from Acts is so quiet, we could easily miss its significance if we don't pause to consider it. Peter had come a long way from the self-assertive disciple who characteristically sought center-stage adulation. The Peter who loved to be in the spotlight was now perfectly willing to stand in Christ's shadow. And his attitude seems to me the real key to learning contentment. When we yield ourselves, in the way Peter did, to the Spirit's prime mission of exalting Christ in all situations of life, we'll shift our eyes from ourselves to God's kingdom and righteousness. And we'll find ourselves learning contentment in all circumstances.

Notes:

1. Dennis E. Johnson, *The Message of Acts in the History of Redemption* (Phillipsburg, N. J.: P&R Publishing, 1997), 58.

2. Edward Donnelly, *Peter, Eyewitness to His Majesty* (Carlisle, Penn.: The Banner of Truth Trust, 1998), 74, 76.

3. Ibid, 58.

Review Questions

1. Briefly explain the statement, "Pentecost was a new creation." Cite several examples from Peter's life (recorded in Acts 1-12) to illustrate your explanation.

2. Read Romans 6:4-7, 11-18, 8:9; 1 Corinthians 12:13; Ephesians 4:30, 5:18; and 1 Thessalonians 5:19. Then use what you learn from these verses to explain the difference between being *born of the Spirit* and being *filled by the Spirit*. Also explain the *importance* of being filled with the Spirit.

3. What evidence is presented in Acts 1-11 that Peter's natural abilities had been retooled and redirected by God's Holy Spirit?

4. Cite one or more examples of how Peter wisely *applied* Spirit-given insight in daily-life situations. Then define the word "wisdom" in your own words.

5. How does Peter reflect newly created contentment in Acts 12:1-17?

6. Do you see evidence in Acts 1-12 of any other newly created qualities in Peter (in addition to courage, wisdom, and contentment)? If so, describe them.

Applying the Word

1. This week review the verses you have memorized from previous lessons. Then begin memorizing one or more of the following:

    Acts 4:12
    2 Corinthians 5:17
    1 Peter 5:6-7

2. D. Martyn Lloyd-Jones said: "We are all so diplomatic, we are all so concerned about dignity, we are all so concerned about being 'scholarly' and not causing offense; we are all so afraid of fanaticism! We do not pray today that preachers may speak 'boldly,' we prefer that they should speak ecumenically....The result is that the people do not know what the Gospel is....We are so much afraid of offending people that we tend to hold back the truth; and so the Christian faith is in jeopardy at this hour." (D. Martyn Lloyd-Jones, *The Christian Soldier: Ephesians 6:10-20* [Grand Rapids, Mich.: Baker Book House, 1977], 360.) Consider Dr. Lloyd-Jones's words in the light of Acts 4:1-30. Do his words convict you of your own lack of boldness? Do they convict you about the type of preaching that you like to hear? Do they convict you about your failure to pray for boldness in your own ministry and in the ministry of your pastor? If so, confess your sins in accord with 1 John 1:9 and then commit to pray regularly for boldness for yourself and for others who proclaim the Gospel.

3. Explain how Peter's example of wise, relevant preaching will help you proclaim the Gospel effectively in your sphere of influence.

4. Read Philippians 4:4-20 carefully and prayerfully. What do each of the following verses teach you about learning contentment: 4, 6-7, 8-9, 12-13, 17, 18, 19, 20? (HINT: Each verse or passage contains an element of contentment that we need to learn. For example, verse 4 emphasizes *joy* and verse 18 emphasizes *thankfulness* as ingredients of contentment.) Would you describe yourself as a content person? If you answered yes, ask a close friend or relative (someone who will be honest with you!) if they also consider you to be a content person. If you are truly content and reflect contentment to others, thank God in prayer for helping you develop this quality which greatly glorifies Him. If you are not content or if you do not reflect contentment to others, meditate on the verses listed above and determine which of their lessons you need to learn. Then ask a leader of your church, or a mature Christian friend, relative, or mentor to help you learn them.

Digging Deeper

1. Carefully read Peter's Gospel proclamations recorded in Acts 2:14-40, 3:12-26, 4:8-12, 5:29-32, and 10:28-43. As you read, note to whom Peter was speaking and record the main points of each proclamation. Describe the similarities and differences of the five proclamations, and then explain how Peter adapted his *presentation* of the Gospel message to his audience without altering the *message* itself. What does his example teach you about proclaiming the Gospel to the people with whom you associate on a daily basis?

*"The mirrors must be finely polished
that are designed
to reflect the image of Christ."*

A. B. Bruce

Chapter 13

Friends Don't Let Friends Live Hypocritically

*(Bible reading: Proverbs 27:5-6; Matthew 6:1-24, 23:1-36;
Acts 15:1-35; Galatians 1:11-2:21; 1 Peter 2:1-12)*

Peter, the mature Christian saint we see depicted in Acts, had a good grip on the Gospel. He understood that Christ's work of atonement was not just for the Jews, but "for all who are far off, as many as the Lord our God shall call to Himself" (Acts 2:39). The vision he had received from the Lord on a rooftop in Joppa had taught him that "God is not one to show partiality, but in every nation the man who fears Him and does what is right, is welcome to Him" (10:34-35). He had witnessed God's Spirit descend upon Jews, Samaritans, and Gentiles alike (2:1-4; 8:14-17; 10:44-48), and had consequently discarded his Jewish exclusiveness. Peter freely welcomed as brethren those Gentiles and Samaritans whom God called to Himself, and did not expect them to conform to Jewish customs and practices.

However, not all Jewish converts had Peter's insight and open-heartedness. Many believed that since redemption in

Christ had come through the Jews, adherence to Judaism was an essential ingredient of Christian conversion. Some of these "Judaizers" were quite influential and unabashedly vocal. Scripture tells us that one gutsy group arrived in Antioch while Peter was there, claimed to be "from James,"[1] and began teaching the brethren "unless you are circumcised according to the custom of Moses, you cannot be saved" (Acts 15:1; Galatians 2:12).

In my mind's eye, I see a bunch of those brethren running to tell Peter what the Judaizers were saying. They all knew that their leader placed no Jewish requirements on Christianity and even shared meals with uncircumcised Gentiles. They all knew that the fisherman had received visions from God advising him that the old covenant racial distinctions were no longer valid, and that he had submitted himself to God's revelation. They all knew that Peter had been empowered by the Spirit to boldly proclaim the Gospel, and that he offered it *freely* to all men and women. Therefore, I'm sure they expected him to boldly tackle the Judaizers and pummel their dastardly doctrine into the ground.

Sadly however, those brethren would be disappointed. Paul tells us in Galatians that Peter allowed himself to be intimidated by this particular group and not only refused to confront them but also "began to withdraw and hold himself aloof" from his Gentile associates (Galatians 2:12). Naturally (and tragically) his behavior made quite an impact on the Antioch church. Paul says that "the rest of the Jews...even Barnabas" were "carried away" and "joined him in hypocrisy" (v. 13).

Hypocrisy: An Equal Opportunity Temptation

Were you as shocked as I was by Peter's behavior? The first time I read this account in Galatians, I assumed that Paul was discussing some other Peter! I didn't want to believe that the "big fisherman" I admired and revered would do such a thing. Sure, Peter had lots of rough edges when he met the Lord, but he had been saved and indwelt by God's Holy Spirit. He had been chosen by God and uniquely equipped to lead the first century church. He had walked with the Lord, learned to humble himself, and displayed newly-created courage, wisdom, and contentment. Peter, of all people, should have been immune to hypocrisy!

However, as I dug more deeply into this passage, I realized that he wasn't. Like all sterling leaders, he had feet of clay and couldn't balance for long up on a pedestal. Although he was chosen of God, saved by grace, and empowered to serve, he was still very human and thus open and vulnerable to the most heinous of sins. Peter's surprising behavior had but one explanation. He failed to take heed when he thought he was standing and consequently fell over a temptation he wasn't expecting (1 Corinthians 10:12).

Peter, like most of us, was prone to man-pleasing.[2] As we have seen in several lessons, his most spectacular failures can be laid at the door of this particular weakness. My guess is that he didn't appreciate the insidiousness of man-pleasing until it led him to deny his Lord. The intensity of his resulting grief could have been due in part to suddenly seeing the seriousness of this character flaw. After receiving the grace of full restoration, Peter's deep gratitude most likely inspired him to carefully guard against repetition of this kind of sin. However, once he had experienced the new creation of Pentecost, he may well have thought that his weakness had been thoroughly conquered. He may well have taken his new Spirit-filled boldness in the face of opponents as positive proof that he had at long last *overcome* his man-pleasing proclivities. And consequently, he may well have let down his guard.

Therefore, when the Judaizers hit town, displayed bogus credentials, and proclaimed "another gospel," Peter not only declined to refute them, but behaved in a way that lent tacit support to what they were saying. As John MacArthur expressed it, "When the winds of legalism blew in, he adjusted his sails accordingly and was blown along with them."[3]

Peter knew what hypocrisy was, and he knew it was something that he should avoid. He had heard Jesus denounce the scribes and Pharisees as those who "say things, and do not do them" (Matthew 23:2-3). He had heard Jesus go on to condemn them as those who embezzle God's glory in ostentatious displays of fraudulent piety (vv. 4-7). And he had also heard Jesus warn His disciples *not to be like these hypocrites* (Matthew 6:1-16; Luke 6:42). And yet Peter withdrew from his Gentile associates even though he believed that he should fellowship with them. He elevated his own prestige and acceptance above the glory of God. He did precisely what Jesus warned him against. And with his man-pleasing guard down, he failed to see the disjunction between his beliefs and his actions.

Peter was in need of a friend indeed — someone who would show him his error and help him correct it — a friend who loved him enough to refuse to allow him to live hypocritically.

Friends Indeed Help Friends In Need

Friends indeed aren't the ones who always agree with you. They're the ones who care enough to go get you when you wander off course. That's the kind of friend Peter had in Paul the Apostle. When Paul saw that Peter was not being "straightforward about the truth of the Gospel," he "opposed him to his face...in the presence of all" (Galatians 2:11, 14). Although Paul's primary concern in his confrontation of Peter was *the truth of the Gospel*, we can also be sure that he was concerned about Peter. Scripture indicates that the two men regarded each other highly (Galatians 2:6-9; 2 Peter 3:15-16) and thus would have been eager to help one another walk worthy of their high calling in Christ.

Paul wasn't out to get Peter when he confronted him publicly. He wasn't jealous, or vengeful, or grinding a pet theological ax. Rather, he was being the very best kind of friend. He had been blessed with the insight to see Peter's man-pleasing behavior as an outright denial of the Gospel's key principle of justification by grace alone through faith alone. And he recognized the disastrous potential of allowing a man in Peter's position to stand uncorrected. Peter's powerful influence had already begun to lead people astray, and if Paul had not acted decisively (and publicly), God's fledgling church would have soon found itself in the direst of straits.

The issue at stake was not minor nor trivial. It was what Martin Luther referred to as "the truth of the gospel....the principle article of all Christian doctrine, wherein the knowledge of all godliness consisteth."[4] With characteristic Lutheran phraseology he went on to affirm, "Most necessary it is, therefore, that we should know this article well, teach

it unto others, and beat it into their heads continually."[5]
Martin Luther had obviously learned from the Apostle Paul
that "if this article of justification be once lost, then all true
Christian doctrine is lost."[6]

Allow Me to Beat This Into Your Head

When God chose to act in love, mercy, and grace to save
chosen sinners, He had no "Plan B." There was only one
way that sinners could be saved from their sin, and that
was within the context of God's invincible holiness. Since
His Law represents and reflects that invincible holiness,
God *could not* extend love, mercy, and grace to those He
had chosen by *canceling or overlooking* the requirements of
His holy Law. God could save fallen sinners *in no other way*
than by fulfilling the requirements of His Law through the
work of a *Substitute.*

God sent His Son, Jesus Christ, the Second Person of the
Trinity, to be that Substitute. As such, He fulfilled all the
righteous demands of God's Law in our place, and then
paid the Law's penalty for all of our sins. God reconciled
His relationship with us by giving us credit for Christ's
perfect obedience to the Law, and by forgiving us for our
sins because of Christ's death on the Cross. You may have
heard Bible teachers or theologians talk about Christ's active
and passive obedience and the doctrine of imputation.
Christ's substitutionary work of atonement is what they
were addressing.

Christ's active obedience refers to His perfect keeping
of God's Law as a man living on earth; and His passive
obedience refers to His paying the Law's prescribed penalty
for sin. *Both* were necessary for sinners to be saved. If Christ
had done nothing but die for our sins, He would not have

completely fulfilled the demands of God's Law in our place. He would have wiped out our guilt and made us innocent of breaking the Law; however, making us innocent would not have made us righteousness. Righteousness results from *obeying* God's Law, not from simply being forgiven for breaking it.[7]

Scripture is clear that reconciliation with God requires that sinners be made not only innocent, but also righteous. Paul tells us that Abraham was reconciled to God when his faith was counted to him as righteousness (Romans 4:22). Paul also says that when we are adopted by God as His children, we receive a "new self" which has been created in righteousness (Ephesians 4:24).

But Paul is also quite clear in Philippians 3:9 that the righteousness that reconciles us to God is not our own righteousness; it is Christ's righteousness. Paul says that his (Paul's) righteousness did not come by his keeping the Law, but that it comes from God through faith in Christ. In Romans 5:17, he explains that God gave him (and gives all Christians) the righteousness that Christ earned as our Substitute when we respond in faith to the truth of the Gospel. In other words, God doesn't merely forgive us because Christ paid the Law's penalty for our sins. God also gives us credit for the righteousness Christ earned as our Substitute by His perfect obedience to God's holy Law.

Christ's work saves us because it perfectly fulfills all the demands of God's Law: it paid in full the Law's penalty against our sin, and it earned for us the credit we need for active obedience. This is what theologians are talking about when they use the word *imputation*. Second Corinthians

5:20-21 describes it quite well. Those verses say that we are reconciled to God because He made Christ, "who knew no sin to be sin on our behalf, that we might become the righteousness of God in Him."

Justice For All...And Mercy For Some

The doctrine of justification views Christ's work of atonement from the viewpoint of a law court. When we enter a law court, either as a litigant or an observer, we expect to see justice served. You know as well as I do that justice is not always served in human law courts, but God's Law Court is different.

Justice can be simply defined as carrying out the requirements of law. Pure justice isn't swayed by things like pity, mercy, or extenuating circumstances. It simply looks at the requirements set forth in the statutes and carries them out without exception. We rarely see an example of pure justice in human legal systems. In our systems, the written statutes seem to be only a starting point. Most successful attorneys seem to build their cases as much on persuasion, sympathy, exculpatory reasons, or excuses as they do on the law.

However, God isn't able to do that because He is holy. He wrote the Law that sinners have broken. That Law consists of righteous requirements that we must obey, and righteous penalties that must be met when we fail to obey. Because those righteous requirements and penalties reflect God's holy character and nature, He is not free to overlook any of them.

If He were to disregard, or even bend, any part of His Law just a little in an effort to show love, mercy, and grace to guilty sinners, He would mar His own holiness and cease to be God. In order for God's holiness to be preserved as He shows love, mercy, and grace to His children, justice has to be served. And Christ's substitutionary work on our behalf does precisely that. Since Christ obeyed the requirements of God's Law perfectly and paid the penalty for the sins of the elect, God is able to pour out love, mercy, and grace on His children without marring His holiness. Christ's work justifies us before God as it transfers our guilt to Christ and transfers His righteousness to us. When Christ lived and died in our place, the requirements of God's Law were all met. Justice was served through imputation, and we were declared righteous in God's sight.

In another sense, Christ's work also "justifies" God as it displays the context of holiness within which salvation occurs. Because of what Christ has done, no one can successfully bring a charge against God, claiming that His plan of salvation is *unjust*. The Atonement of Christ assures that justice is served when sinners are saved and places salvation wholly within the bounds of God's invincible holiness.

People do frequently argue that God acts *unfairly* when He chooses some but not all for salvation; however these folks are not addressing the issue of justice. Rather, their cry of unfairness usually reveals a mistaken concept of grace. God's invincible holiness requires Him to act justly, but it doesn't require that He extend mercy to anyone. God's holiness would not have been marred even slightly if He had required all sinners to pay the penalty for breaking His Law. He would have been perfectly justified in sending every sinner to Hell and starting over again. But He chose not to do that. Instead, He chose to display His own glory *more fully* by redeeming some fallen sinners from bondage to sin. That choice required Him to redeem *the sinners He chose* within the context of His holiness, but it did not require Him to redeem *all* fallen sinners.

Salvation is gracious — unmerited favor, undeserved mercy. Salvation is not required of God, nor is it merited by us. God's holiness was not affected by the number of sinners He chose to save, but it would have been compromised if He had not saved those He chose in accord with the demands of His Law.

Peter Responds to Paul's Admonition

Paul doesn't tell us in Galatians how Peter responded to his admonition; however, Peter himself makes it clear in his first epistle that he heard his friend out and got back on track. Writing to persecuted believers scattered throughout Pontus, Galatia, Cappadocia, Asia, and Bithynia, he declares:

> *Therefore, putting aside all malice and all guile and hypocrisy and envy and all slander, like newborn babes, long for the pure milk of the word, that by it you may grow in respect to salvation, if you have tasted the kindness of the Lord. And coming to Him as to a living stone, rejected by men, but choice and precious in the sight of God, you also, as living stones, are being built up as a spiritual house for a holy priesthood, to offer up spiritual sacrifices acceptable to God through Jesus Christ....But you are a chosen race, a royal priesthood, a holy nation, a people for God's own possession, that you may proclaim the excellencies of Him who has called you*

out of darkness into His marvelous light; for you once were not a people, but now you are the people of God; you had not received mercy, but now you have received mercy. (1 Peter 2:1-5, 9-10)

We see no hint of exclusiveness in these verses — no fear of open alignment with Gentile believers — no man-pleasing attempt to add Jewish rites to Christ's work of atonement. Peter's example illustrates clearly that the goal of our sanctification is obedience to Jesus Christ (1 Peter 1:2), which often involves humbly submitting ourselves to correction from others.

Of all the *Footprints of the Fisherman* that we have examined in this study, I have a hunch that this one may be the hardest to follow. Most of us quickly bristle when we are corrected by others. We hate being confronted with our sinful behavior, and we despise admitting that we were dead wrong. We bend over backwards to justify what we've done and to point out that overlooked log in the eye of our accuser. We get so concerned about maintaining our "image" that we resist God-inspired efforts to enhance our Christlikeness.

Therefore, if we want to walk worthy of our high calling in Christ (and we do!), we desperately need to heed Peter's example. As you work through the following exercises, ask God to help you examine yourself for hypocrisy — even if that means using a friend to confront you. Then beseech Him to give you the grace to humbly submit to correction.

Notes:

1. Acts 15:24 may indicate that James *later* denied that these Judaizers spoke on his authority. Commentators and scholars disagree about whether the Jerusalem Council took place before or after the incident recorded in Galatians 2:11-14. I tend to agree with those who think that it followed Paul's confrontation of Peter. For well reasoned arguments for both positions, see John Stott, *The Bible Speaks Today: The Message of Galatians.* Downers Grove, Ill.: InterVarsity Press, 1968 (original title: *Only One Way*), and William Hendriksen, *New Testament Commentary: Galatians, Ephesians, Philippians, Colossians, and Philemon.* Grand Rapids, Mich.: Baker Books, 1968.

2. For an insightful and truly helpful analysis of the insidious sin of man-pleasing, see Edward T. Welch, *When People are Big and God is Small: Overcoming Peer Pressure, Codependency, and the Fear of Man.* Phillipsburg, N. J.: P&R Publishing, 1997.

3. John MacArthur Jr., *The MacArthur New Testament Commentary: Galatians* (Chicago: Moody Press, 1987), 55.

4. John Stott, *The Bible Speaks Today: The Message of Galatians* (Downers Grove, Ill.: InterVarsity Press, 1968), 59. (original title: *Only One Way*).

5. Ibid.

6. Ibid.

7. For a deeper discussion of this critical doctrine, see R. C. Sproul's tape series, *The Drama of Redemption* and *The Cross of Christ*, available from Ligonier Ministries, P.O. Box 547500, Orlando, FL 32854.

Review Questions

1. Read Acts 2:38-39 and Acts 10:1-11:18. What evidence do you see in these verses that Peter understood the true nature of the Gospel?

2. In light of your answer to review question 1, explain the hypocritical nature of Peter's behavior described in Galatians 2:12-13.

3. Read Matthew 23:1-36 and summarize, in your own words, Jesus' description of the hypocritical scribes and Pharisees. Then read Matthew 6:1-24 and summarize, in your own words, Jesus' warnings to His disciples. Finally, relate Peter's behavior in Galatians 2:12-13 to Jesus' words in these Matthew passages.

4. How did Paul behave as a friend indeed to Peter? Explain the importance of Paul's behaving this way.

5. Explain the necessity of Christ's substitutionary work of atonement.

6. Define, in your own words, the doctrine of justification. Read Romans 9:14-29. Does God act either unjustly or unfairly when He chooses some but not all for salvation? Explain your answer.

7. Read through Peter's first epistle and cite evidence that Peter responded in a God-honoring manner to Paul's admonition.

Applying the Word

1. Devote this week to reviewing all the verses you have memorized in previous lessons.

2. In Matthew 23, Jesus characterized the hypocritical scribes and Pharisees as those who "do all their deeds to be noticed by men" (v. 5) and then went on to describe some of their specific hypocritical practices: (1) They refused to accept God's way of salvation and then worked hard to convince others to reject it also (v. 13); (2) They worked night and day to sell "private label" religion and to make disciples who would carry on their tradition (v. 15); (3) They elevated financial gain above genuine worship of God (v. 16); (4) They scrupulously adhered to religious rules while ignoring the heart attitudes that gave meaning to such obedience (v. 23); (5) They deceitfully presented an appearance of purity, promise, and beauty to cover their evil intent of robbery and self-indulgence (v. 25); (6) They carefully maintained a veneer of holiness as a covering for their rotting souls (v. 27); and (7) They paid lip service to great servants of God while doing everything possible to dismantle the fruits of their efforts (v. 29).

    Study Jesus' teaching in Matthew 23 along with His words of warning to His disciples in Matthew 6:1-24. Then ask God to use these passages of Scripture to help you examine yourself for evidence of hypocritical living. (Psalm 139:23-24 would be a good prayer pattern.) Ask Him to make you willing to receive correction from others if necessary so that any areas of hypocrisy in your life can be corrected. Once these areas are revealed to you, determine what steps you must take to eliminate them, and then make a plan to help you do what needs to be done. Seek support and help from your pastor, one of your church leaders, or a mature Christian friend if you sense a need to be held accountable for carrying through with your plan.

3. Review the lessons in this study and describe one or more significant things you have learned from Peter's example. How will what you have learned change the way that you live day by day?

Digging Deeper

1. A.B. Bruce said, "The mirrors must be finely polished that are designed to reflect the image of Christ." Obviously, Peter was one of those mirrors. Explain in your own words how Paul's confrontation of Peter in Galatians 2:11-21 was part of his "polishing process."

Recommended Reading

Boice, James Montgomery, *Christ's Call to Discipleship*. Chicago: Moody Press, 1986.

Bridges, Jerry, *The Joy of Fearing God*. Colorado Springs, Colo.: Waterbrook Press, 1997.

Bruce, A. B., *The Training of the Twelve*. Grand Rapids, Mich.: Kregel Publications, 1971, 1988.

Carson, D. A., *The Difficult Doctrine of the Love of God*. Wheaton, Ill.: Crossway Books, 2000.

Donnelly, Edward, *Peter: Eyewitness of His Majesty*. Carlisle, Penn.: The Banner of Truth Trust, 1998.

Gaffin, Richard B. Jr., *Perspectives on Pentecost: New Testament Teaching on the Gifts of the Holy Spirit*. Phillipsburg, N. J.: Presbyterian and Reformed Publishing Co., 1979.

Johnson, Dennis E., *The Message of Acts in the History of Redemption*. Phillipsburg, N. J.: P & R Publishing, 1997.

Martin, Hugh, *Simon Peter*. Carlisle, Penn.: The Banner of Truth Trust, 1967, 1984. (First published in *The Family Treasury* during 1869.)

MacArthur, John Jr., *The Freedom and Power of Forgiveness.* Wheaton, Ill.: Crossway Books, 1998.

_____, *The Love of God.* Dallas: Word Publishing, 1996.

Owen, J. Glyn, *From Simon to Peter.* Welwyn, England: Evangelical Press, 1985.

Sande, Ken, *The Peacemaker: A Biblical Guide to Resolving Personal Conflict.* Grand Rapids, Mich.: Baker Book House, 1991.

Sproul, R. C., *Grace Unknown: The Heart of Reformed Theology.* Grand Rapids, Mich.: Baker Books, 1997.

_____, *Chosen By God.* Wheaton, Ill.: Tyndale House Publishers, Inc., 1986.

Welch, Edward T., *When People Are Big and God is Small.* Phillipsburg, N.J.: P&R Publishing, 1997.

Appendix A

What Must I Do to Be Saved?

A strange sound drifted through the Philippian jail as midnight approached. It was the sound of human voices—but not the expected groans of the two men who earlier had been beaten with rods and fastened in stocks. Rather, the peaceful singing of praises to their God floated through the cells.

While the other prisoners quietly listened to them, the jailer dozed off, content with the bizarre calm generated by these two preachers, who had stirred so much commotion in the city just hours before.

Suddenly a deafening roar filled the prison, and the ground began to shake violently. Sturdy doors convulsed and popped open. Chains snapped and fell at prisoners' feet. Startled into full wakefulness, the jailer stared, horrified, at the wide-open doors that guaranteed his prisoners' escape—and his own death. Under Roman law, jailers paid with their lives when prisoners escaped. Resolutely, he drew his sword, thinking it better to die by his own hand than by Roman execution.

"Stop! Don't harm yourself—we are all here!" a voice boomed from the darkened inner cell. The jailer called for lights and was astonished to discover his prisoners standing quietly amid their broken chains. Trembling with fear, he rushed in and fell at the feet of the two preachers. As soon as he was able, he led them out of the ruined prison and asked in utter astonishment, "Sirs, what must I do to be saved?"

In the entire history of the world, no one has ever asked a more important question. The jailer's words that day may well have been motivated by his critical physical need, but the response of Paul and Silas addressed his even more critical spiritual need: "Believe in the Lord Jesus, and you shall be saved, you and your household."[1]

If you have never "believed in the Lord Jesus," your spiritual need, just like the jailer's, is critical. As long as your life is stained with sin, God cannot receive you into His presence. The Bible says that sin has placed a separation between you and God (Isaiah 59:2). It goes on to say that your nature has been so permeated by sin that you no longer have any desire to serve and obey God (Romans 3:10–12); therefore, you are not likely to recognize or care that a separation exists. Your situation is truly desperate because those who are separated from God will spend eternity in hell.

Since your sinful nature is unresponsive to God, the only way you can be saved from your desperate situation is for God to take the initiative. And this He has done! Even though all men and women deserve the punishment of hell because of their sin, God's love has prompted Him to save some who will serve Him in obedience. He did this by sending His Son, the Lord Jesus Christ, to remove the barrier of sin between God and His chosen ones (Colossians 2:13–14).

What is there about Jesus that enables Him to do this? First of all, He is God. While He was on earth He said, "He who has seen Me has seen the Father" (John 14:9) and "I and the Father are one" (John 10:30). Because He said these things, you must conclude one of three things about His true identity: (1) He was a lunatic who believed he was God when he really wasn't; (2) He was a liar who was willing to die a hideous death for what he knew was a lie; or (3) His words are true and He is God.

Lunatics don't live the way Jesus did, and liars don't die the way He did; so if the Bible's account of Jesus' life and words is true, you can be sure He *is* God.

Since Jesus is God, He is perfectly righteous and holy. God's perfect righteousness and holiness demands that sin be punished (Ezekiel 18:4), and Jesus' perfect righteousness and holiness qualified Him to bear the punishment for the sins of those who will be saved (Romans 6:23). Jesus is the only person who never committed a sin; therefore, the punishment He bore when He died on the cross could be accepted by God as satisfaction of His justice in regard to the sins of others.

If someone you love commits a crime and is sentenced to die, you may offer to die in his place. However, if you also have committed crimes worthy of death, your death cannot satisfy the law's demands for your crimes *and* your loved one's. You can die in his place only if you are innocent of any wrongdoing.

Since Jesus lived a perfect life, God's justice could be satisfied by allowing Him to die for the sins of those who will be saved. Because God is perfectly righteous and holy, He could not act in love at the expense of justice. By sending Jesus to die, God demonstrated His love *by acting to satisfy His own justice* (Romans 3:26).

Jesus did more than die, however; He also rose from the dead. By raising Jesus from the dead, God declared that He had accepted Jesus' death in the place of those who will be saved. Because Jesus lives eternally with God, those for whom Jesus died can be assured that they also will spend eternity in heaven (John 14:1–3). The separation of sin has been removed!

Ah, but the all-important question remains unanswered: What must *you do* to be saved? If God has sent His Son into the world for sinners, and Jesus Christ died in their place, what is left for you to do? You must respond in faith to what God has done. This is what Paul meant when he told the jailer, "Believe in the Lord Jesus, and you shall be saved."

Believing in the Lord Jesus demands three responses from you: (1) an understanding of the facts regarding your hopeless sinful condition and God's action to remove the sin barrier that separates you from Him; (2) acceptance of those facts as true and applicable to you; and (3) a willingness to trust and depend upon God to save you from sin. This involves willingly placing yourself under His authority and acknowledging His sovereign right to rule over you.

But, you say, how can I do this if sin has eliminated my ability to know and appreciate God's work on my behalf? Rest assured that if you desire to have the sin barrier that separates you from God removed, He already is working to change your natural inability to respond. He is extending His gracious offer of salvation to you and will give you the faith to receive it.

If you believe that God is working to call you to Himself, read the words He has written to you in the Bible (perhaps beginning with the book of John in the New Testament) and pray that His Holy Spirit will help you understand what is written there. Continue to read and pray until you are ready to *repent*—that is, to turn away from sin and commit yourself to serving God.

Is there any other way you can be saved? God Himself says no, there is not. The Bible He wrote says that Jesus is the only way in which the sin barrier between you and God can be removed (John 14:6; Acts 4:12). He is your hope, and He is your *only* hope.

If you have questions or need any help in this matter, please write to The Evangelism Team, Providence Presbyterian Church, P. O. Box 14651, Albuquerque, NM 87191, before the day is over. God has said in His Bible that a day of judgment is coming, and after that day no one will be saved (Acts 17:30–31; 2 Thessalonians 1:7–9). The time to act is now.

---

[1] For a full biblical account of this event, see Acts 16:11–40.

Appendix B

What Is the Reformed Faith?

The term *the Reformed Faith*[1] can be defined as a theology that describes and explains the sovereign God's revelation of His actions in history to glorify Himself by redeeming selected men and women from the just consequences of their self-inflicted depravity.

It is first and foremost *theology* (the study of God), not *anthropology* (the study of man). Reformed thinking concentrates on developing a true knowledge of God that serves as the necessary context for all other knowledge. It affirms that the created world, including humanity itself, cannot be accurately understood apart from its relationship with the Creator.

The Reformed Faith describes and explains God's revelation of Himself and His actions to humanity; it does not consist of people's attempts to define God as they wish. The Reformed Faith asserts that God has revealed Himself in two distinct ways: He reveals His existence, wisdom, and power through the created universe—a process known as *natural revelation* (Romans 1:18–32); and He reveals His requirements and plans for mankind through His written Word, the Bible—a process known as *special revelation* (2 Timothy 3:16–17).

Reformed theologians uphold the Bible as the inspired, infallible, inerrant, authoritative, and fully sufficient communication of truth from God to humanity. When they call the Bible *inspired*, they mean that the Bible was actually written by God through the agency of human authorship in a miraculous way that preserved the thoughts of God from the taint of human sinfulness (2 Peter 1:20–21). When they call the Bible *infallible*, they mean that it is *incapable* of error. When they call it *inerrant*, they mean that the Bible, *in actual fact*, contains no errors. The Bible is authoritative because it comes from God, whose authority over His creation is absolute (Isaiah 46:9–10). And it is completely sufficient because it contains everything necessary for us to know and live according to God's requirements (2 Peter 1:3–4).

By studying God's revelation of Himself and His work, Reformed theologians have learned two foundational truths that structure their thinking about God's relationship with human beings: God is absolutely sovereign, and people are totally depraved.[2]

Reformed thought affirms that God, by definition, is absolutely sovereign—that is, He controls and superintends every circumstance of life, either by direct miraculous intervention or by the ordinary outworking of His providence. Reformed theologians understand that a "god" who is not sovereign cannot be God because his power would not be absolute. Since the Reformed Faith accepts the Bible's teaching regarding the sovereignty of God, it denies that *anything* occurs outside of God's control.

The Reformed Faith affirms the biblical teaching that Adam was created with the ability to sin and that he chose to sin by disobeying a clear command of God (Genesis 3:1–7).

Choosing to sin changed basic human nature and left us unable not to sin—or *totally depraved*. Total depravity does not mean that all people are as bad as they possibly could be, but that every facet of their character is tainted with sin, leaving them incapable and undesirous of fellowship with God. The Reformed Faith denies that totally depraved men and women have any ability to seek after or submit to God of their own free will. Left to themselves, totally depraved men and women will remain out of fellowship with God for all eternity.

The only way for any of these men and women to have their fellowship with God restored is for God Himself to take the initiative. And the Bible declares that He has graciously chosen to do so (John 14:16). *For His own glory,* He has chosen some of those depraved men and women to live in fellowship with Him. His choice is determined by His own good pleasure and not by any virtue in the ones He has chosen. For this reason, *grace* is defined in Reformed thought as "unmerited favor."

God accomplished the salvation of His chosen ones by sending His Son, the Lord Jesus Christ, to bear God's righteous wrath against sin so that He could forgive those He had chosen. Even though Christ's work was perfect and complete, its effectiveness is limited to those who are chosen by God for salvation. Christ would not have been required to suffer any more or any less had a different number been chosen for redemption, but the benefit of His suffering is applied only to those who are called by God to believe in Him. And all those who are effectually called by God eventually will believe and be saved, even though they may resist for a time (John 6:37). They cannot forfeit the salvation they have received (John 10:27–30; Romans 8:31–39).

Reformed thought affirms the clear teaching of the Bible that salvation is by faith alone through Christ alone (John 14:6; Acts 4:12; Ephesians 2:8–9) and that human works play no part in salvation although they are generated by it (Ephesians 2:10). Salvation transforms a person's nature, giving him or her the ability and the desire to serve and obey God. The unresponsive heart of stone is changed into a sensitive heart of flesh that responds readily to God's voice (Ezekiel 36:25–27) and desires to glorify Him out of gratitude for the indescribable gift of salvation.

Reformed thought affirms that God works in history to redeem His chosen ones through a series of covenants. These covenants define His Law, assess penalties for breaking His Law, and provide for the imputation of Jesus' vicarious fulfillment of God's requirements to those God intends to redeem.[3]

The Reformed Faith affirms that we were created and exist solely to glorify God, and it denies that God exists to serve us. It affirms that God acts to glorify Himself by putting His attributes on display and that His self-glorifying actions are thoroughly righteous since He is the only Being in creation worthy of glorification. It denies that God is motivated to act *primarily* by man's needs; rather, it affirms that all of God's actions are motivated *primarily* for His own glory.

The Reformed Faith emerged as a distinct belief system during the sixteenth and seventeenth centuries when men like Luther, Calvin, Zwingli, and Knox fought against the Roman Catholic Church to restore Christian doctrine to biblical truth. These men were labeled *Reformers*, but they would have been better labeled *Restorers* since their goal was to correct abuses and distortions of Christianity that were rampant in the established Roman church. Reformed thinkers since their day have sought to align their own understanding of God and His actions in history as closely as possible to His revealed truth.

[1] This brief overview of basic Reformed beliefs is not intended to be a full explanation of or apologetic for the Reformed Faith. For a more detailed description and analysis of the Reformed Faith see: R. C. Sproul, *Grace Unknown* (Grand Rapids: Baker Books, 1997); Loraine Boettner, *The Reformed Faith* (Phillipsburg, N.J.: Presbyterian and Reformed, 1983); *Back to Basics: Rediscovering the Richness of the Reformed Faith,* ed. David G. Hagopian (Phillipsburg, N.J.: P & R Publishing, 1996); *The Westminster Confession of Faith* (with its accompanying Catechisms); or the theological writings of John Calvin, B. B. Warfield, Charles Hodge, and Louis Berkhof.

[2] Both of these truths are taught throughout the pages of Scripture; however, the sovereignty of God can be seen very clearly in Isaiah 40–60 and in Job 38–42, while the total depravity of man is described quite graphically in Romans 3:10–18.

[3] An excellent discussion of these covenants is contained in Chapter 5 of R. C. Sproul, *Grace Unknown.*

The Purpose of Deo Volente Publishing

"And do not be conformed to this world,
but be transformed by the renewing of your mind,
that you may prove what is that good and
acceptable and perfect will of God"
Romans 12:2 (NKJV)

Deo Volente Publishing exists to help make the exhortation of Romans 12:2 a living, daily reality in the believer's life.

Our goal is:
- to edify believers in Christ,
- to encourage non-conformity to the world's standards,
- to exhort believers to live radically transformed lives that reflect the knowledge, enjoyment and practice of what is good, acceptable, and perfect in God's sight.

We will endeavor to meet our goal by publishing material that:
- is consistently Reformed in theology,
- is intensely practical for a daily Christian walk,
- encourages holy living in every aspect of life through the reforming power of God's Word.

DEO VOLENTE
PUBLISHING
P.O. BOX 4847
LOS ALAMOS, NM   87544
Phone: (505)672-1622

FAX: (505)672-1615